STUDENT

VITAL PURSUITS:

CHASING WHAT'S TRUE

Connect with God. Connect with others.
Connect with life.

LIFE CONNECTIONS® YOUTH

SERENDIPITY HOUSE

Vital Pursuits Youth Edition: Chasing What's True
Student Book

Published by Serendipity House Publishers
Nashville, Tennessee

ISBN: 1-5749-4245-X

Dewey Decimal Classification: 248.83
Subject Headings:
SPIRITUAL LIFE \ YOUTH--RELIGIOUS LIFE

To purchase additional copies of this resource or other studies:
ORDER ONLINE at www.SerendipityHouse.com
WRITE Serendipity House, 117 10th Avenue North, Nashville, TN 37234
FAX (615) 277-8181
PHONE (800) 525-9563

1-800-525-9563
www.SerendipityHouse.com

Printed in the United States of America
13 12 11 10 09 08 07 06 1 2 3 4 5 6 7 8 9 10

CONTENTS

SESSION 1
Speak Up: Talking to God 7

SESSION 2
Listen Up: Listening to God 17

SESSION 3
Plug In: Connecting to a Spiritual Community 27

SESSION 4
Tap In: Worshipping God 37

SESSION 5
Open Up: Giving to God 47

SESSION 6
Time Trial: Spending a Daily Time with God 57

SESSION 7
Heads Up: How to Study God's Word 65

SESSION 8
Fill Up: Meditating and Memorizing God's Word 75

SESSION 9
Word Up: Applying God's Word to My Life 83

SESSION 10
Game On: Living in the Power of the Spirit 93

SESSION 11
Power Up: Resisting Temptation 103

SESSION 12
Over the Top: Overcoming Doubt 111

SESSION 13
Decision Time: Serving God with My Life 119

Acknowledgments 127
Group Directory 128

EXPERIENCE

Combine ***teaching that engages a large-group*** with ***dynamic small-group experiences and discussions*** and you end up grappling with reality and experiencing real life change. Throughout 13 sessions, you will find power in just being together and connecting.

Get Ready

To get the most from this experience, spend some time with God each day leading up to your group session. Wrap your brain around the short Bible passages, listen to God, and jot down thoughts and insights.

LifePoint

Your large-group leader will welcome everyone. You'll hear the "LifePoint" or big idea for the session, and then divide into small groups.

Say What?

Enjoy fun,interactive experiences and discussions in your small group. Discuss the "Random Question of the Week" and join activities or discussions that lead into session topic.

So What?

The Master Teacher will lead the entire group in understanding what God has to say on the topic. Content is deep, but engaging. Follow along, jot notes, and respond to questions in your book.

Do What?

All study should direct us toward action and life change. It's easier and more helpful to discuss application in small groups. The goal is to be real with each other in order to connect with God and each other. Find power in the support and prayers of others in the group.

Now What?

To see real power in life, you don't want to leave the session and just go on as normal. The "Now What?" assignments help you continue your journey and give you an opportunity to go deeper with God.

At A Glance

Get Ready

Daily time with God
& your journal

LifePoint

Large Group:
Welcome & Theme

Say What?

Small Group:
Fun & Interaction

So What?

Large Group:
Teaching & Discovery
(Master Teacher)

Do What?

Small Group:
Getting Real
& Connecting

Now What?

Continue your journey...

GROUP COVENANT

It is important that your group covenant together, agreeing to live out important group values. Once these values are agreed upon, your group will be on its way to experiencing Christian community. It's very important that your group discuss these values—preferably as you begin this study. The first session would be most appropriate. (Check the rules to which each member of your group agrees.)

- ☑ Priority: While you are in this course of study, you give the group meetings priority.
- ☑ Participation: Everyone is encouraged to participate and no one dominates.
- ☑ Respect: Everyone is given the right to his or her own opinion, and all questions are encouraged and respected.
- ☑ Confidentiality: Anything that is said in the meeting is never repeated outside the meeting.
- ☑ Life Change: We will regularly assess our own life-change goals and encourage one another in our pursuit of becoming more like Christ.
- ☑ Empty Chair: The group stays open to reaching new people at every meeting.
- ☑ Care and Support: Permission is given to call upon each other at any time, especially in times of crisis. The group will provide care for every member.
- ☑ Accountability: We agree to let the members of the group hold us accountable to the commitments we make in whatever loving ways we decide upon.
- ☑ Mission: We will do everything in our power to start a new group.
- ☑ Ministry: Members of the group will encourage one another to volunteer and serve in a ministry and to support missions by giving financially and/or personally serving.

Session

1

SPEAK UP: TALKING TO GOD

Get Ready

Read one these short Bible passages each day and spend a few minutes wrapping your brain around it. Be sure to jot down any insights you discover.

MONDAY

Read Matthew 6:5-6

In this verse, Jesus describes the hypocrites who prayed out loud only to be seen in public. Where is your favorite place to pray? Why do you pray?

My faverite place is outside and the church because God is in charge of nature. I pray for people who are ill and for protection, and to ask for forgivness

TUESDAY

Read Matthew 6:7-8

Do you think God knows your needs? How does this passage give you hope?

Yes I do but you need to ask him. Because God really listens to your prays and you have to do it a certain way.

WEDNESDAY

Read Matthew 6:9-10

In which area of your life are you willing to pray God's will be done? In which areas are you hesitant to pray that prayer? Why?

When I'm confused I ask for God's will be done. When I'm really confident in doing somthing I want my oan will.

THURSDAY

Read Matthew 6:11-13

Who do you need to forgive? Why? Is there someone you need to ask to forgive you?

Many people but Brittny because I haven't forgiven her for leaving me alone and not talking to me. She also needs to forgive me because I thought wrong of her.

FRIDAY

Read Psalm 139:23-24

In what ways does God know your heart? Ask God to show you other areas of your life that need His touch. He knows my heart by knowing what I need and want.

SATURDAY

Read Mark 7:24-30

The mother in this passage falls at Jesus' feet as she asks Jesus to remove the demons from her daughter. How do you approach God in prayer? Are you like this woman? Explain. I approach God as closing my eyes and folding my hands. Yes and no because I dont have a daughter how's possesed by a deamon. And I dont see the Lord. But I know he's there

SUNDAY

Read Philippians 4:6-7

What do you feel anxious or stressed about? Does knowing that God is in control help? How? losing Grandpa was stressing. Yes because I know he left when God wanted him too.

LifePoint

God longs for a relationship with each of us. Prayer is one of the most—if not the most—basic means by which we can continue the conversation that He initiated at our beginning.

SMALL-GROUP TIME: Divide into smaller groups of 4-8, preferably in a circle. You will have a small-group leader for "Say What?"

Say What? (15 MINUTES)

1

Random Question of the Week:

What does it mean when a gorilla sticks his tongue out?

Group Experience: Uniquely You

You will participate in a guessing game led by your small-group leader.

1. The way to pray 1. Praise God and thank him
2. Confess your sins and tell him your needs and concerns.
3. Pray for the people in your life

LARGE-GROUP TIME: Turn to face the front for this teaching time. Follow along and ake notes in your *Student Books.*

So What? (30 MINUTES)

Beginning the Conversation

1. What is one of the most common but least effective motivators to pray?
Should

Learning from the Bible ...

Matthew 6:5-13

Learning from the Bible

5 "Whenever you pray, you must not be like the hypocrites, because they love to pray standing in the synagogues and on the street corners to be seen by people. I assure you: They've got their reward! 6 But when you pray, go into your private room, shut your door, and pray to your Father who is in secret. And your Father who sees in secret will reward you. 7 When you pray, don't babble like the idolaters, since they imagine they'll be heard for their many words. 8 Don't be like them, because your Father knows the things you need before you ask Him.

9 "Therefore, you should pray like this:
Our Father in heaven,
Your name be honored as holy.
10 Your kingdom come.
Your will be done
on earth as it is in heaven.
11 Give us today our daily bread.
12 And forgive us our debts,
as we also have forgiven our debtors.
13 And do not bring us into temptation,
but deliver us from the evil one.
For Yours is the kingdom and the power
and the glory forever. • Amen.

LARGE-GROUP TIME: Your leader will share some key points with you. Follow along and take notes in your *Student Books.*

Discovering What to Say

2. Give one solid biblical reason why we should talk to God.

~~Praise~~ confeuss my sins

3. Why would God want you to talk about Him during prayer?

4. If God knows what you have done wrong, why do you need to confess it?

1

Important Aspects of Prayer

5. What three aspects of prayer are identified in the Matthew passage?

1. praise God for who he is
2. confess your sins
3. Give Thanks
4. Share your life
5. Make supplications for yourself and other people

SMALL-GROUP TIME: Small-group leaders will direct your discussions. Everyone will gain more if you are open and honest in responding to questions.

Do What? (15 MINUTES)

Group Experience: ACTS Acrostic

A ttributes ______ Start your prayer by recognizing characteristics of God. What are three of your favorite things about God?

1. He is The Almighty
2. He knows everything
3. Loves everyone

C onfess ______ Next, admit your struggles, challenges, and failures and recognize that this distorts your ability to hear and understand God's voice in your life.

T hanks giving ______ Take the time to thank God for all he has done for you. What are you most thankful for today? Why?

That we got cheese and turkey for our Sandwiches

S upplications ______ Make your requests (supplications) for other people.

LIFEPOINT REVIEW

God longs for a relationship with each of us. Prayer is one of the most—if not the most—basic means by which we can continue the conversation that He initiated at our beginning.

"Do Points"

These "Do" Points will help you grab hold of this week's LifePoint. Be open and honest as you answer the questions within your small group.

1

1. Establish a close relationship with God through prayer. You won't be close to someone you don't talk to. Commit to spend a consistent time with the Lord in prayer.
   What will you do to make your prayer time a priority?

2. Manage stress, anxiety, and worry with prayer. Most people run to friends immediately when panic strikes. Determine today to take your worries and concerns to God first.
   Why is it better to take your stress and worries straight to God?

3. Develop an organized prayer list to use when praying for others. You will keep up with things better when you are organized. Create a plan for organization. Some suggestions for good planning include starting and being consistent with a journal, maintaining an online list with daily reminders, or tracking your prayer life using index cards.
   Share your ideas about how to get organized with the group.

Prayer Connection:

Now is the time to get that prayer list started! Lets encourage, support and pray for each other in our journeys to connect to God through prayer.

Share prayer needs with the group, especially those that are related to today's lesson. Your group facilitator will close your time in prayer.

Prayer Needs:

Remember your "Get Ready" daily Bible readings and questions at the beginning of Session 2.

now What?

Take it to the next level by completing one of these assignments this week:

Option #1:
Get to know God better by learning more of the names used in the Bible for Him. Research the many different names people in the Old Testament used to refer to God. Make a list of those names as well as what each name meant. Pray using the different names of God.

Option #2:
Memorize Philippians 4:6-7 to help you manage your stress and worries. Every time you are tempted to stress out or worry, quote these verses aloud and let God take control.

Option #3:
Every time you see a prayer of yours answered, make a note of it on your prayer list. Over time this will become your own testimony to God's work in your life through prayer.

Bible Reference Notes

Use these notes to deepen your understanding as you study the Bible on your own:

Matthew 6:5

they love to pray standing in the synagogues and on street corners. Jesus is not making a blanket condemnation of public prayer. Devout, sincere Jews prayed three times a day. Nothing was wrong with standing to pray, even in public, for this was the standard posture for prayer among Jews. There are many examples of sincere and passionate public prayers recorded in Scripture. Jesus was challenging the motive of their public prayer.

1

to be seen by men. Jesus identified the motive of some public prayers as religion for show. The goal: Obtain the approval of observers. Note Jesus' similar call for sincere motives in charitable giving and fasting (Matt. 6:1–4,16–18). The motive behind Ananias' and Sapphira's false report of their property sale was to impress others with their supposed sacrifice (Acts 4:32–5:11). We should be glad God does not so expose our impure motives.

Matthew 6:6

go into your room. Some translations say "closet." The word can also refer to a storeroom. The location provides privacy for an audience of One.
your Father ... will reward you. Our tendency is to equate reward with some type of material prize. The phrase may best be translated "respond to you" (see Hebrews 11:6: "He rewards those who earnestly seek him").

Matthew 6:7

babbling like pagans, for they think they will be heard because of their many words. The Greek verb *battalogeo* is unique in biblical and secular literature. No use of the word is known beyond this verse. It is rather difficult to translate into English. William Tyndale was the first to translate the word as babble. The Revised Standard Version's rendering "heap up empty phrases" resonates with the criticism of a mindless and mechanical flood of words. It is the sincerity and passion of our words that engages God.

Matthew 6:8

your Father knows what you need before you ask him. Why pray and ask if God already knows what we need? Understanding God's omniscience should not undermine the necessity of asking. James penned, "You do not have, because you do not ask God" (4:2). We never inform an all-knowing God of anything. Nevertheless, His complete awareness of our needs does not eliminate the order of God's kingdom: Ask, seek, and knock. Neither a rambling monologue of eloquence nor a filibuster of mechanical prayer will impress God or weary Him into submission. Jesus' use of the phrase "your Father" is a further reminder that God is not reluctant to respond but is sensitive to the needs of His children.

NOTES

Session

2

LISTEN UP: LISTENING TO GOD

2

Get Ready

Read one these short Bible passages each day and spend a few minutes wrapping your brain around it. Be sure to jot down any insights you discover.

MONDAY

Read 1 Samuel 3:1-3

This passage states that in those days, the Word of the Lord was rare. How rare is the Word of the Lord in your life? In what ways are you exposed to the Word daily or weekly? 2 a week not including bible study or bible school

TUESDAY

Read 1 Samuel 3:4

Samuel doesn't realize that God is speaking to him. He thinks Eli is calling him. How do you know when God is speaking to you? What would your reply be if He called your name in the night? I would probaly think it was Daddy. But it would be scary but I would know because the dogs didn't bark.

WEDNESDAY

Read 1 Samuel 3:5-7

Think of a time when you understood something in the Bible because God revealed it to you in some way. How does it feel to know that the God of the universe wants to reveal Himself to you?

THURSDAY

Read 1 Samuel 3:8-9

Eli is Samuel's spiritual mentor in this passage. To whom do you go for advice about spiritual things?

FRIDAY

Read 1 Samuel 3:10-14

Samuel responds to God with a spirit of listening. God knows your name and asks you to listen to Him. How do you listen for God?

SATURDAY

Read 1 Samuel 3:15

How can hearing from God have a calming effect? How might hearing from God make you uncomfortable?

SUNDAY

Read 1 Samuel 3:16-20

How do people around you know that you are a follower of Jesus? Why or why not?

LifePoint

God has always revealed Himself to us and He continues to speak today. We must be available and able to hear His voice through the channels He chooses to use.

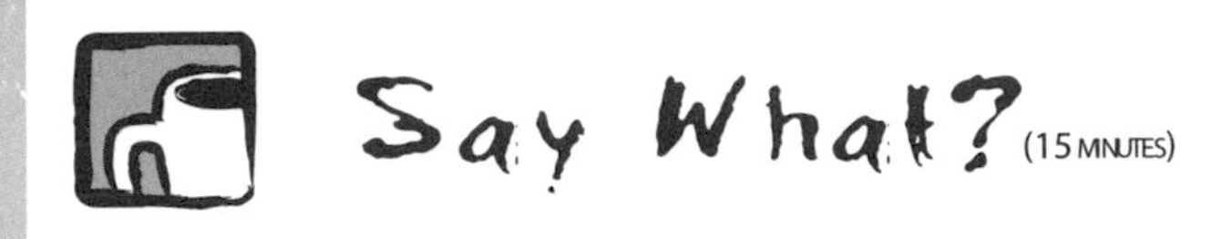

SMALL-GROUP TIME: Divide into smaller groups of 4-8, preferably in a circle. You will have a small-group leader for "Say What?"

Random Question of the Week:

If you could add a face to Mount Rushmore, who would you add?

Group Experience: Listen Up!

You will participate in a listening experiment led by your small-group leader.

After the experiment, discuss the following questions:

1. What happened to the student's ability to hear "God" as the noise level increased?

2. What are some of the major "noises" in your life that sometimes distract you or keep you from hearing from God?

3. If "1" represents "I can't hear God at all" and "10" is "I hear Him loud and clear," how would you rate yourself?

OPTIONAL QUESTIONS

1. How were you able recognize some of the voices?

2. What elements of your physical environment helped or hindered your ability to recognize the voices?

3. What things are necessary for you to distinguish voices you recognize from voices that you don't? For example, how much does it help to have a relationship with the person?

LARGE-GROUP TIME: Turn to face the front for this teaching time. Follow along and take notes in your *Student Books.*

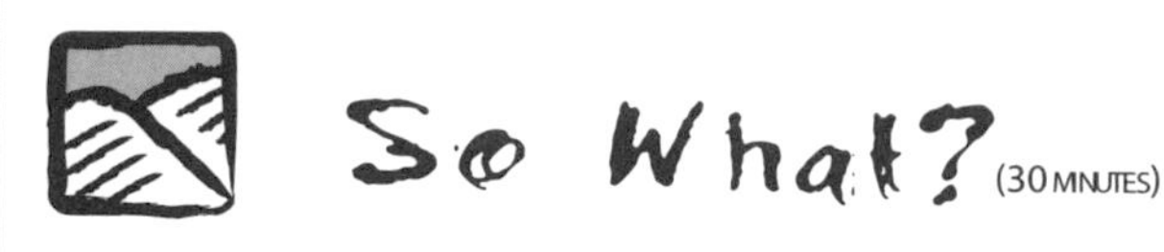

God Still Speaks

1. What are three good questions to ask when you think about listening to God?

   Question 1: ______________________________.

   Question 2: ______________________________.

   Question 3: ______________________________.

Learning from the Bible

Learning from the Bible ...

1 Samuel 3:1-20

[1] The boy Samuel served the LORD in Eli's presence. In those days the word of the LORD was rare and prophetic visions were not widespread.

[2] One day Eli, whose eyesight was failing, was lying in his room. [3] Before the lamp of God had gone out, Samuel was lying down in the tabernacle of the LORD where the ark of God was located.

[4] Then the LORD called Samuel, and he answered, "Here I am." [5] He ran to Eli and said, "Here I am; you called me."

"I didn't call," Eli replied. "Go and lie down." So he went and lay down.

[6] Once again the LORD called, "Samuel!"

Samuel got up, went to Eli, and said, "Here I am; you called me."

"I didn't call, my son," he replied. "Go and lie down."

[7] Now Samuel had not yet experienced the LORD, because the word of the LORD had not yet been revealed to him. [8] Once again, for the third time, the LORD called Samuel. He got up, went to Eli, and said, "Here I am; you called me."

Then Eli understood that the LORD was calling the boy. [9] He told Samuel, "Go and lie down. If He calls you, say, 'Speak, LORD, for Your servant is listening.' " So Samuel went and lay down in his place.

[10] The LORD came, stood there, and called as before, "Samuel, Samuel!"

Samuel responded, "Speak, for Your servant is listening."

[11] The LORD said to Samuel, "I am about to do something in Israel that everyone who hears about it will shudder. On that day I will carry out against Eli everything I said about his family, from beginning to end. [13] I told him that I am going to judge his family forever because of the iniquity he knows about: his sons are defiling the sanctuary, and he has not stopped them. [14] Therefore, I have sworn to Eli's family: The iniquity of Eli's family will

never be wiped out by either sacrifice or offering."

[15] Samuel lay down until the morning; then he opened the doors of the LORD's house. He was afraid to tell Eli the vision, [16] but Eli called him and said, "Samuel, my son."

"Here I am," answered Samuel.

[17] "What was the message He gave you?" Eli asked. "Don't hide it from me. May God punish you and do so severely if you hide anything from me that He told you." [18] So Samuel told him everything and did not hide anything from him. Eli responded, "He is the LORD. He will do what He thinks is good."

[19] Samuel grew, and the LORD was with him and let nothing he said prove false. [20] All Israel from Dan to Beer-sheba knew that Samuel was a confirmed prophet of the LORD.

2

LARGE-GROUP TIME:
Your leader will share some key points with you. Follow along and take notes in your *Student Books.*

Creative Conversations

2. What are some of the dramatic and creative ways that God has spoken to people in the Bible?

3. What are the primary ways that God speaks to people today?

Learning to Listen

4. How can you prepare to listen to God?

5. What three things can you seek that will help you to hear from God?

6. Why is confession important to listening?

Confirming the Source

7. What is one definite signal that what you are sensing or hearing isn't from God?

8. How can other people help you to confirm that you really did hear from God?

SMALL-GROUP TIME: Small-group leaders will direct your discussions. Everyone will gain more if you are open and honest in responding to questions.

Do What? *(15 MINUTES)*

Group Experience: Radio Active

1. In what ways is listening to God similar to listening for radio waves?
you have to be quite you have to have the Equipment

2. Check the statement that best describes you right now. Why?
   - ☐ I never hear from God
   - ☐ I hear God, but I don't understand Him
   - ☐ I don't even have a radio
   - ☐ All I get is static
   - ☑ I usually hear what God is saying to me
   - ☐ I feel like He talks to me, but I'm scared to respond in case I am wrong
   - ☑ Other Hearing him is hard and I somtimes don't hear him

3. What is the greatest obstacle in your life to hearing from God?
   - ☑ I'm not still; I can't slow down long enough
   - ☐ I lack solitude; I am never alone
   - ☐ I lack silence; I don't like it quiet
   - ☐ Other ______

4. Which area of your life do you want to hear from God about?
   - ☑ Personal ☑ School
   - ☑ Family ☑ Dating
   - ☑ Future ☑ Friends
   - ☑ Other all other areas

LIFEPOINT REVIEW

God has always revealed Himself to us and He continues to speak today. We must be available and able to hear His voice through the channels He chooses to use.

"Do" Points

These "Do" Points will help you grab hold of this week's LifePoint. Be open and honest as you answer the questions within your small group.

1. Set aside time to be still long enough to hear God. Your schedule may be busy, but it is worth it to make listening to God a priority. **When will you commit to being still and listening each day?**

   yes!

2. Choose solitude in order to listen to God. It can be difficult to find alone time to hear from God.
   When will you be able to get by yourself and spend time with God?

   when I'm in my Room

3. Become comfortable with silence by going without music or television for a set period each day. It is possible to teach yourself to be O.K. with no noise.
   How will your relationship with God change if you set aside quiet time each day to listen?
   We could hear better

Prayer Connection:

This is the time to encourage, support, and pray for each other in our journeys to learn to hear from God.

Share prayer needs with the group, especially those that are related to hearing from God. Your group facilitator will close your time in prayer.

Prayer Needs:

Remember your "Get Ready" daily Bible readings and questions at the beginning of Session 3.

Now What?

Continue on the path of spiritual growth by choosing one of the following assignments to complete this week:

Option #1:

Learn how to listen to God in silence by fasting from various forms of media this week. A fast is when you purposely do without something. Replace whatever you've chosen to fast from with spending time with God through prayer or Bible study. Set aside a specific amount of time. Decide which types of media you will give up and take that time to talk and listen to God.

Option #2:

Interview people about how they hear from God. Survey people around you and ask them to share the most common way they usually hear God speak to them. Keep a list of the responses you receive and continue to track how and when you hear from God. Take time to thank Him for speaking to you.

Bible Reference Notes

Use these notes to deepen your understanding as you study the Bible on your own:

1 Samuel 3:1

The boy Samuel ministered before the Lord under Eli. First Samuel talks of the remarkable conception of Samuel to a barren Hannah and her dedication of Samuel to the Lord. Hannah releases her weaned son to the care of the priest Eli who would mentor him in the service of God in the temple. Most commentators agree that Samuel was at least 12 years old at the time of this episode.
In those days the word of the Lord was rare; there were not many visions. During the period of the judges and prior to Samuel's calling, there were very few people who received a direct revelation from God

2

1 Samuel 3:3

The lamp of God had not yet gone out. This speaks of the golden lampstand in the temple's Holy Place. The phrase is meant to indicate the lateness of the hour prior to sunrise. It was a violation of one's priestly duties to allow the lamp to go out before morning.

1 Samuel 3:7

Samuel did not yet know the Lord. Mentored by Eli, Samuel certainly knew much about God and was genuine in his worship and service to God. The phrase implies that up until now Samuel had no direct experience with God such as receiving a revelation (note the parallel to God speaking to Moses at the burning bush). The latter part of verse 7 ("the word of the Lord had not yet been revealed to him") provides further clarification.

1 Samuel 3:9

Speak, Lord, for your servant is listening. Samuel identifies himself as a servant, communicating to God that He is poised to receive and submit to God's message.

1 Samuel 3:11

will make the ears of everyone who hears of it tingle. God's action will seize the attention of everyone who hears of it.

1 Samuel 3:13

the sin he knew about. First Samuel 2 reveals that Eli's grown sons, active servants in the temple "had no regard for the Lord" (v. 12). They "were treating the Lord's offering with contempt" (v. 17), and "slept with the women who served at the entrance to the Tent of Meeting" (v. 22). Chapter 2 reveals that Eli became aware of these evil deeds and while he warned his sons, he did not hold them accountable or discipline them. Eli's sons ignored the warning.

1 Samuel 3:14

The guilt of Eli's house will never be atoned for by sacrifice or offering. God's mind was made up and would not be changed by any ceremony or ritual. Years later the prophet Samuel would declare to King Saul, "Does the Lord delight in burnt offerings and sacrifices as much as in obeying the voice of the Lord? To obey is better than sacrifice, and to heed is better than the fat of rams" (1 Sam. 15:22).

1 Samuel 3:18

l***et him do what is good in his eyes.*** As painful as the consequences would be for him personally as a priest and father, Eli acknowledged the perfect right God has to act in accordance with His perfect sovereignty.

1 Samuel 3:19

he [God] let none of his [Samuel's] words fall to the ground. God ensured that all of Samuel's words and proclamations proved reliable. Because of this, Samuel was recognized as a prophet who spoke the word of the Lord.

NOTES

Session

3

PLUG IN: CONNECTING TO A SPIRITUAL COMMUNITY

Get Ready

3

Read one of these short Bible passages each day and spend a few minutes wrapping your brain around it. Be sure to jot down any insights you discover.

MONDAY

Read Acts 2:42-43

Amazing things began to happen in the early church once they committed themselves to God and to each other. How has the teaching, passion, and devotion at your church impacted your spiritual growth?

TUESDAY

Read Acts 2:44-45

The early believers met the needs in their community. In what ways do you give to others in your church and community?

WEDNESDAY

Read Acts 2:46

How does fellowship with other believers affect you? In what ways do you offer your fellowship to others and how do you hope others to be affected by it?

THURSDAY

Read Acts 2:47

The result of this Christian community was that others were led to Christ. Think about the moment you understood salvation and accepted Jesus as your Savior. Remember to thank God and praise Him this week for your rescue.

FRIDAY

Read Romans 12:10

What does it mean to show someone honor? How can you love someone in a "brotherly" way?

SATURDAY

Read Ecclesiastes 4:9-12

When was the last time you helped a fellow believer? Who do you know right now that stumbled but has no one to lift him up? How can you help?

SUNDAY

Read Proverbs 27:17

How have Christian friends "sharpened" you? How do you help sharpen others?

LifePoint

We were not created to live life alone! Instead, we have been created to journey with others. Being a part of a Christian community is essential to our spiritual growth.

SMALL-GROUP TIME: Divide into smaller groups of 4-8, preferably in a circle. You will have a small-group leader for "Say What?"

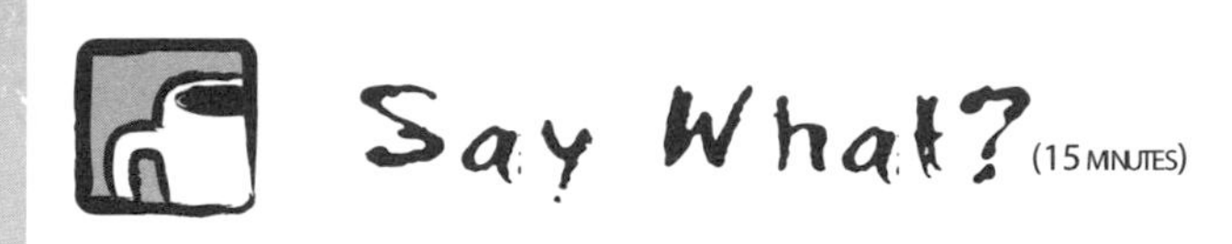

Random Question of the Week:

What would make a group of stray dogs stay together?

Group Experience: My Neighborhood

You will participate in a drawing activity led by your small-group leader.

After everyone has finished drawing, discuss the following questions:

1. What is your favorite part of the community?

2. What do the lines mean? What significance do they have?

3. List two things that connect you to people.

LARGE-GROUP TIME: Turn to face the front for this teaching time. Follow along and take notes in your *Student Books.*

A Great Example

1. What determines if members feel pushed or connected with a community?

2. What is a sign of a spiritually healthy person?

Learning from the Bible

Learning from the Bible ...

Acts 2:42-47

42 And they devoted themselves to the apostles' teaching, to fellowship, to the breaking of bread, and to prayers.

43 Then fear came over everyone, and many wonders and signs were being performed through the apostles. 44 Now all the believers were together and had everything in common. 45 So they sold their possessions and property and distributed the proceeds to all, as anyone had a need. 46 And every day they devoted themselves [to meeting] together in the temple complex, and broke bread from house to house. They ate their food with gladness and simplicity of heart, 47 praising God and having favor with all the people. And every day the Lord added to them those who were being saved.

LARGE-GROUP TIME: Your leader will share some key points with you. Follow along and take notes in your *Student Books.*

The Priority of Spiritual Community

3. Devotion = _________________ + ____________________.

4. How did the Acts 2 spiritual community demonstrate devotion?

The Purpose of Spiritual Community

5. What are the purposes of spiritual community?

   A. ______________________________ of God's Word

   B. ______________________________together

   C. ______________________________for each other

   D. Responding to ______________________________of members

   E. ______________________________ the relationships

   F. Attracting people from ______________________________ the church

The Benefits of Spiritual Community

6. What are some of the benefits of genuine spiritual community?

   A.

   B.

   C.

   D.

7. How do you build an effective community?

3

SMALL-GROUP TIME: Small-group leaders will direct your discussions. Everyone will gain more if you are open and honest in responding to questions.

Do What? (15 MINUTES)

Group Experience: Like Velcro?

1. Think about your spiritual life as it relates to community. How connected are you? Place an "X" on the line graph below to indicate your response.

○ ○ ○ ○ ○ ○ ○ ○ ○ ○ ○

I am a one sided piece of Velcro — I am completely connected like two sides of Velcro

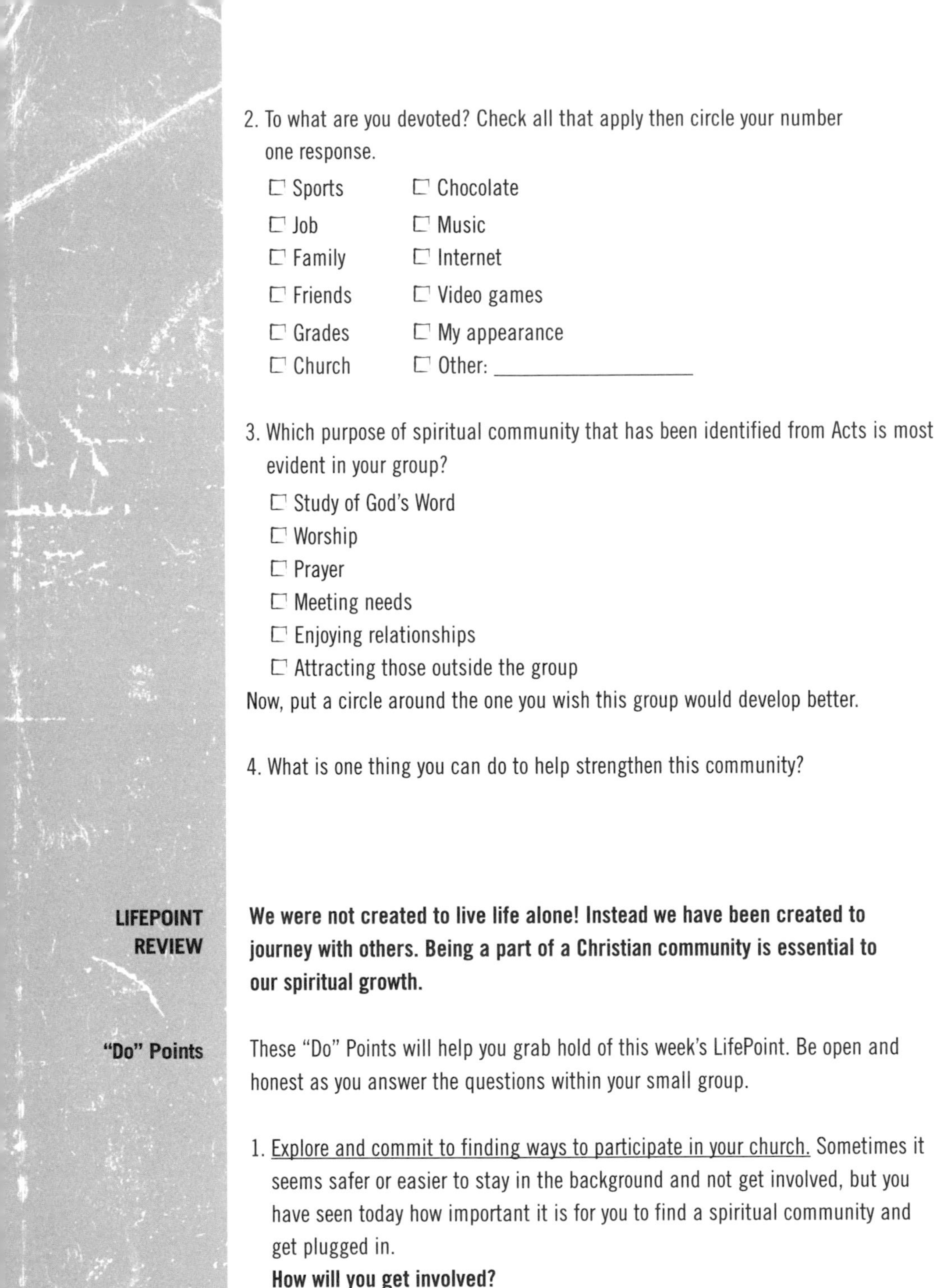

2. To what are you devoted? Check all that apply then circle your number one response.

- ☐ Sports
- ☐ Job
- ☐ Family
- ☐ Friends
- ☐ Grades
- ☐ Church
- ☐ Chocolate
- ☐ Music
- ☐ Internet
- ☐ Video games
- ☐ My appearance
- ☐ Other: ___________________

3. Which purpose of spiritual community that has been identified from Acts is most evident in your group?

- ☐ Study of God's Word
- ☐ Worship
- ☐ Prayer
- ☐ Meeting needs
- ☐ Enjoying relationships
- ☐ Attracting those outside the group

Now, put a circle around the one you wish this group would develop better.

4. What is one thing you can do to help strengthen this community?

LIFEPOINT REVIEW

We were not created to live life alone! Instead we have been created to journey with others. Being a part of a Christian community is essential to our spiritual growth.

"Do" Points

These "Do" Points will help you grab hold of this week's LifePoint. Be open and honest as you answer the questions within your small group.

1. Explore and commit to finding ways to participate in your church. Sometimes it seems safer or easier to stay in the background and not get involved, but you have seen today how important it is for you to find a spiritual community and get plugged in.
   How will you get involved?

2. Commit to actively contributing to a small group. Once you have found the church that God wants you to be part of, it is vital that you get even more involved by getting into a small group.
   If your youth group doesn't have small-groups, what can you do to get small groups started?

3. Begin an accountability relationship with another Christian. This relationship will be a support and encouragement to you – like iron sharpening iron!
   Who could hold you accountable as you continue to grow in your spiritual walk?

3

Prayer Connection:

Now its time to put into action what we have been studying about community.

Share any prayer requests you have with the group and make a note of any that other's share. Your group facilitator will close your time in prayer.

Prayer Needs:

Remember your "Get Ready" daily Bible readings and questions at the beginning of Session 4.

Now What?

Go a little deeper with God in your spiritual journey by completing one of these assignments this week.

Option #1:
Research more about the early church by reading through Acts or by interviewing a pastor or staff member. Make an effort to observe the various communities in your life – athletic teams, clubs, social groups. Keep a journal or list of the characteristics you find.

Option #2:
Reach out to people who are not involved in a spiritual community. Ask questions and discover reasons they have chosen not to be plugged in. Pray for those people. Ask God how you can help implement changes to make your group open and inviting to lost people.

Bible Reference Notes

Use these notes to gain further understanding of the text as you study on your own.

Acts 2:42

the apostles' teaching. As eyewitnesses and followers of Christ, the apostles' teaching about Jesus was considered authoritative and credible. The teaching likely included a recitation of Jesus' words and teaching (Matt. 28:20), accounts of His earthly ministry and miracles, and His crucifixion and resurrection. At the center of this teaching was a proclamation of God's redemptive plan for man through Jesus.

fellowship. *Koinonia*, a favorite word of the apostle Paul, is used only this once in the writings of Luke. The word suggests a unique and intimate sharing that Christians have with God and with one another.

breaking of bread. There is considerable debate among scholars about whether this refers to the Lord's Supper or to a more informal sharing of a meal. Perhaps its placement in the sentence gives us a clue. Note that the other three features mentioned in 2:42 (apostles' teaching, fellowship, and prayer) are spiritually charged activities, implying that the inclusion of the fourth one is also a significant spiritual activity. Therefore, the immediate context of the phrase gives us cause to interpret "breaking of bread" to be a worshipful exercise of commemorating the Lord's Supper.

prayer. Luke uses both the definite article and the plural form, so the most accurate rendering is "the prayers," suggesting formal prayers and prayer times set by the Jerusalem temple leaders. This does not suggest a mere continuation of habit or tradition. The traditional forms of prayer were often filled with new content. It is most probable that this close-knit faith community often practiced a more informal and spontaneous expression of prayer. Most of the references to prayer in the epistles imply a community experience and expression of prayer, rather than a private one.

3

Acts 2:43

many wonders and miraculous signs were done by the apostles. The signs and wonders were done by the apostles for the same two reasons Jesus performed miracles: (1) out of compassion and in response to a need; (2) in order to validate the message and messenger (see Matt. 9:6).

Acts 2:44

had everything in common. This implies that no authority enforced sharing (as in communism). Property and possessions were sold according to need. The sacrifice was generous and voluntary.

Acts 2:46

meet together in the temple courts. The early believers, not entirely detached from their Jewish heritage, continued to make the temple a central place of their spiritual and social lives. Gentile believers, out of respect to Christianity's roots in Judaism, joined their Jewish brothers.

broke bread in their homes. Homes played a significant role in the health and the growth of the early church. The breaking of bread in this context implies a casual, friendly sharing of a meal.

Acts 2:47

enjoying the favor of all the people. The spiritual community won the admiration of observers. Note that this is early in the life of the church and precedes the widespread persecution which would soon follow. However, there is evidence to suggest that there were pockets of persecution in the church's infancy. The generous giving to "anyone as he had need" included those who experienced persecution and suffered economic consequences.

NOTES

Session 4

TAP IN: WORSHIPPING GOD

Get Ready

Read one of these short Bible passages each day and spend a few minutes wrapping your brain around it. Be sure to jot down any insights you discover.

4

MONDAY

Read John 4:19-20

The woman in this passage is asking Jesus about the best place is to worship. In what places do you find worship most meaningful?

TUESDAY

Read John 4:21-22

Although you may worship God often, how well do you really know Him?

WEDNESDAY

Read John 4:23-24

What does it mean to you to worship God "in spirit and in truth"?

THURSDAY

Read John 4:25-26

Is there anything that you wish Jesus would explain to you through worship?

FRIDAY

Read Exodus 20:18-20

What does it mean to have a "fear of God"? How does this fear affect your worship of God?

SATURDAY

Read Matthew 15:8-9

How can you honor God with your lips but fail to honor Him with your heart?

SUNDAY

Read Revelation 4:8-11

How might John's vision of heaven change the way you worship?

LifePoint

God desires to engage with our hearts and minds. The best way for Him to do that is through our worship. God wants you to be an intimate and passionate worshiper.

SMALL-GROUP TIME: Divide into smaller groups of 4-8, preferably in a circle. You will have a small-group leader for "Say What?"

Say What? (15 MINUTES)

Random Question of the Week:

If you melted dry ice, could you swim without getting wet?

Group Experience: Two Truths and a Lie

From the list below, choose two of the sentences to complete truthfully. Then, try to trick the other people in your group by choosing one sentence to answer with a lie. Share your three sentences with the group. Have them try to correctly identify the lie.

One of my favorite snack foods is______________________

I would most like to have a gift certificate from ______________________

If I could have any car, it would be ______________________

My favorite music group is ______________________

More than anyone else, I would most like to meet ______________________

The most exciting thing that ever happened to me was ______________________

____

I have traveled to ______________________

9

LARGE-GROUP TIME: Turn to face the front for this teaching time. Follow along and take notes in your *Student Books.*

So What? (30 MINUTES)

Worshipers Wanted

1. What kind of person is God looking for?

2. What kind of worshiper does God want you to be?

Learning from the Bible ...

Matthew John 4:19-26

LARGE-GROUP TIME:
Your leader will share some key points with you. Follow along and take notes in your *Student Books*.

Learning from the Bible

[19] "Sir," the woman replied, "I see that You are a prophet. [20] Our fathers worshiped on this mountain, yet you [Jews] say that the place to worship is in Jerusalem."
[21] Jesus told her, "Believe Me, woman, an hour is coming when you will worship the Father neither on this mountain nor in Jerusalem. [22] You Samaritans worship what you do not know. We worship what we do know, because salvation is from the Jews. [23] But an hour is coming, and is now here, when the true worshipers will worship the Father in spirit and truth. Yes, the Father wants such people to worship Him. [24] God is spirit, and those who worship Him must worship in spirit and truth."
[25] The woman said to Him, "I know that Messiah is coming" (who is called Christ). "When He comes, He will explain everything to us."
[26] "I am [He]," Jesus told her, "the One speaking to you."

What is Worship?

3. How do the words for worship in the Old and New Testament differ?

Worship in Spirit

4. What does it mean to "worship in Spirit"?

5. Describe heart-engaged worship. What does it look like?

Worship in Truth

6. What does it mean to "worship in truth"?

The Balance of Spirit and Truth

7. Why does balance between spirit and truth matter?

9

SMALL-GROUP TIME: Small-group leaders will direct your discussions. Everyone will gain more if you are open and honest in responding to questions.

Do What? (15 MINUTES)

Group Experience: Top Five List

1. As a group, create a Top Five list of places and/or ways that you have the best, most sincere worship.

   Top Five Ways or Places to Worship in spirit and truth:
   1.
   2.
   3.
   4.
   5.

2. What is it about those places or methods of worship that gets them on the list?

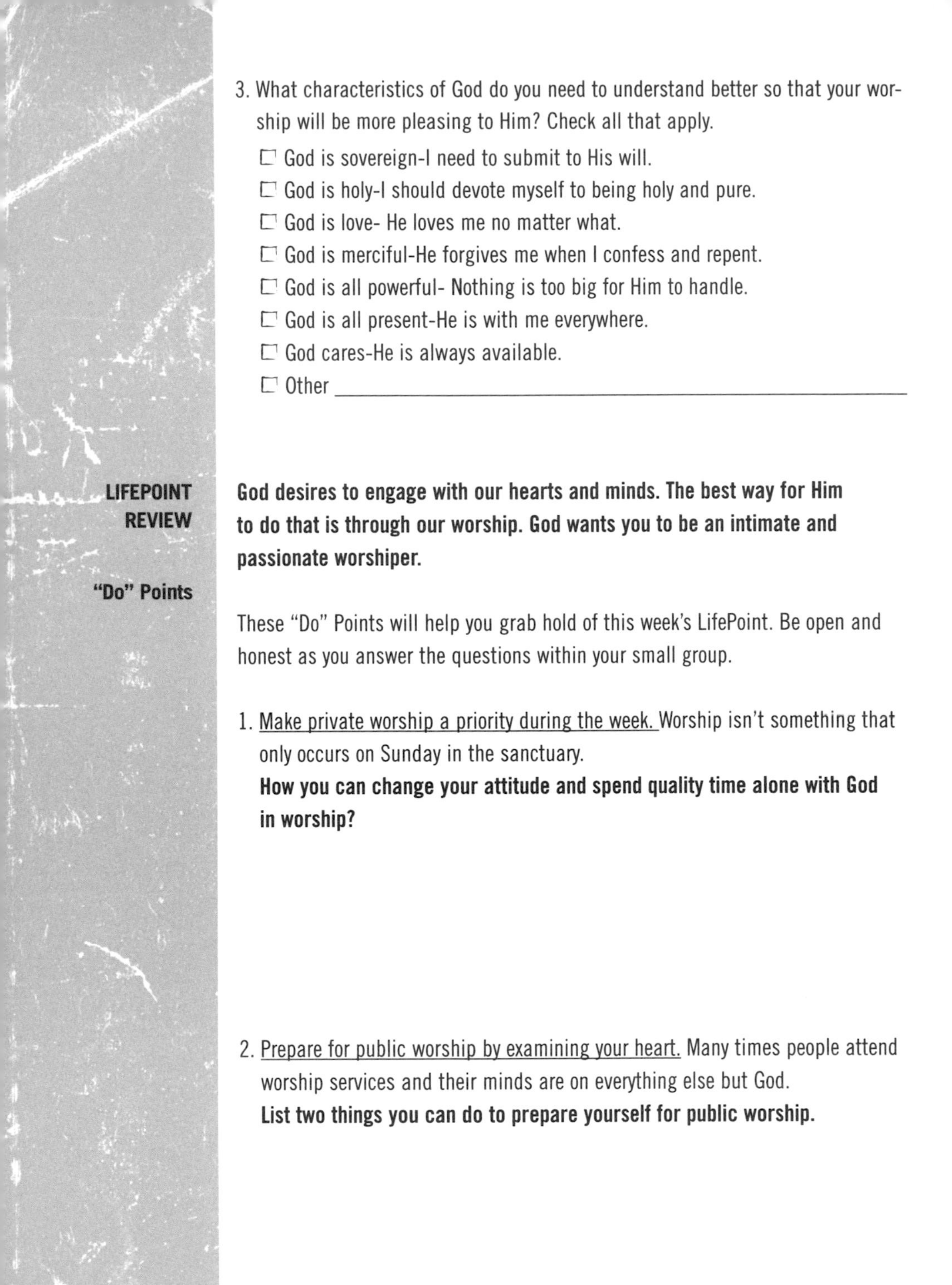

3. What characteristics of God do you need to understand better so that your worship will be more pleasing to Him? Check all that apply.
   - ☐ God is sovereign-I need to submit to His will.
   - ☐ God is holy-I should devote myself to being holy and pure.
   - ☐ God is love- He loves me no matter what.
   - ☐ God is merciful-He forgives me when I confess and repent.
   - ☐ God is all powerful- Nothing is too big for Him to handle.
   - ☐ God is all present-He is with me everywhere.
   - ☐ God cares-He is always available.
   - ☐ Other ______________________________

LIFEPOINT REVIEW

God desires to engage with our hearts and minds. The best way for Him to do that is through our worship. God wants you to be an intimate and passionate worshiper.

"Do" Points

These "Do" Points will help you grab hold of this week's LifePoint. Be open and honest as you answer the questions within your small group.

1. Make private worship a priority during the week. Worship isn't something that only occurs on Sunday in the sanctuary.
   How you can change your attitude and spend quality time alone with God in worship?

2. Prepare for public worship by examining your heart. Many times people attend worship services and their minds are on everything else but God.
   List two things you can do to prepare yourself for public worship.

3. Choose to live a life of worship. We don't just go to worship. We make worship such a part of our lives that we become worshipers.
What does the idea of being a worshiper instead of a person who goes to worship mean to you?

Prayer Connection:

This is the time to encourage, support, and pray for each other in our journeys to become true worshipers.

9

Take time now to encourage and support each another by sharing your prayer concerns and writing down the requests of others in your group. Your facilitator will close your time in prayer.

Prayer Needs:

Remember your "Get Ready" daily Bible readings and questions at the beginning of Session 5.

Continue on the path of spiritual growth by choosing one of the following assignments to complete this week:

Option #1:
Consider different ways that you are aware of people worshiping in your church or other locations in the Bible. Note and make a list of the postures, attitudes, and activities inherent in each instance. Which worship actions interest you most? Try some different ways to worship this week and remember to focus on spirit and truth.

Option #2:
Ask people to share with you the most powerful worship experience they have had. Do more people share about public or private worship? What are some common things you notice about powerful worship experiences?

Bible Reference Notes

Use these notes to gain further understanding of the text as you study on your own.

John 4:19 — ***I can see that you are a prophet.*** Because Jesus is a stranger to the village, the Samaritan woman knows that His full knowledge of her personal history is supernatural.

John 4:20 — ***Our fathers worshiped on this mountain, but you Jews claim that the place where we must worship is in Jerusalem.*** Because the woman is startled by Jesus' knowledge of her and she wants to avoid the subject of her past and present lifestyle, she seeks to detour Jesus into a religious controversy. Instead of derailing Jesus' train of thought, she actually drives the conversation right where Jesus would have it. Around 400 B.C., the Samaritans built a temple on Mount Gerizim because they believed the mountain to be especially sacred as the site of Abraham's and Jacob's altars. Furthermore, when Moses exhorted and warned the people prior to their entry into the promised land (Deut. 27:1–28:68), he ordered that the tribes be divided, half on Mount Ebal and half on Mount Gerizim. In a scripted reading and response, those on Gerizim pronounced the blessings of God while those standing on Mount Ebal were to recite the cursings of God for disobedience. The Samaritans, thus, were certain that Mount Gerizim was the favored location for worship. The Jews insisted that Solomon's commission to build the temple in Jerusalem confirmed that the city was to be the center of worship. So strong was their conviction and so intense was their animosity toward Samaritans that the Jews later destroyed the Gerizim temple which, of course, only increased the hostility between the two groups.

John 4:21 — ***you will worship the Father neither on this mountain nor in Jerusalem.*** Jesus skirts the historical debate and elevates the issue above one of location.

John 4:22 — ***You Samaritans worship what you do not know.*** The Samaritan Bible contained only the Pentateuch (Genesis, Exodus, Leviticus, Numbers, Deuteronomy), and thus their knowledge of God was incomplete. Furthermore, their worship was impure because many Samaritans had integrated foreign deities into their worship.
salvation is from the Jews. The Messiah would be a Jew.

John 4:24 — ***God is spirit.*** If God were corporeal, He would be confined to one place, but if He is noncorporeal as Jesus asserts, God can be worshiped anywhere.
worship in spirit and in truth. The meaning of this phrase is developed rather fully in the session.

John 4:22 — ***Messiah ... will explain everything.*** While she credited Jesus with being a prophet, she considered the matter too complex and important to readily accept Jesus' interpretation and implied that only the Messiah could bring closure to the issue.

John 4:24 — ***I ... am he.*** This is the only occasion before his trial that He openly declared His messiahship. The term did not have the dangerous political overtones in Samaria that it would have in purely Jewish regions. This confession is made early in Jesus' ministry when He was not so well-known.

NOTES

Session

5

OPEN UP: GIVING TO GOD

Get Ready

Read one of these short Bible passages each day and spend a few minutes wrapping your brain around it. Be sure to jot down any insights you discover.

MONDAY

Read Luke 12:13-15

Jesus warns the crowd to be on guard against greed. How can you protect yourself from the dangers of greed?

TUESDAY

Read Luke 12:16-19

The man in the parable is busy getting more stuff. Are you more focused on getting stuff than you are on sharing what you have with others?

WEDNESDAY

Read Luke 12:20-21

What can this parable teach you about your attitude toward money?

THURSDAY

Read Malachi 3:8-10

The people in this passage are robbing from God by not giving to Him. Yet, if they would give, He would bless them. How can failing to give affect you adversely?

FRIDAY

Read 2 Corinthians 8:1-5

Would you say that you have given yourself to God 100%? If not, what are you holding back?

SATURDAY

Read John 12:3-8

Mary performs an act of worship in this passage. What are some other "acts" of worship?

SUNDAY

Read John 3:16

God is the ultimate giver. Describe the impact of God's love and the sacrifice of Jesus on your world.

LifePoint

We give things to people we love . . . flowers, gifts, our time etc. Giving to God is an important element in taking your relationship with God to the next level. Giving expresses worship and love.

SMALL-GROUP TIME: Divide into smaller groups of 4-8, preferably in a circle. You will have a small-group leader for "Say What?"

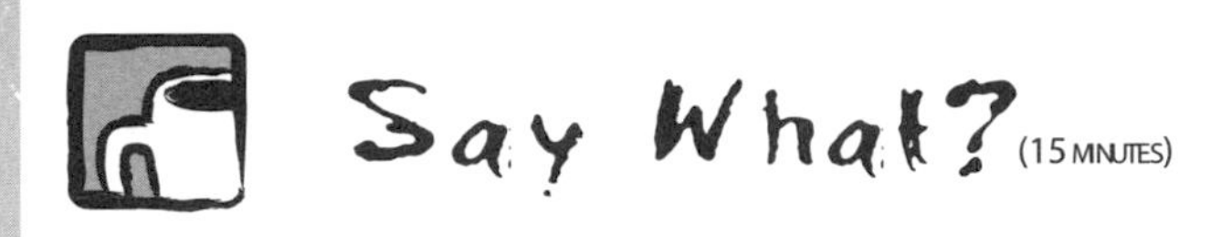

Random Question of the Week:

If someone gave you $100, what is the first thing you would do with it?

Group Experience: Guessing Game

You will participate in a guessing game led by your small-group leader.

After the activity, discuss the following questions:

1. What do you think the last set of items used in the opening had in common with today's LifePoint about giving?

2. Have you ever given someone the perfect gift? If so, what was it? How did that make you feel?

3. Are there more ways to give to God than just money? What else can you give?

LARGE-GROUP TIME: Turn to face the front for this teaching time. Follow along and take notes in your *Student Books.*

So What? (30 MINUTES)

Heart Treasure

1. According to Jesus, what is the surest way to discover where your heart is?

Learning from the Bible ...

Luke 12:13-21

Learning from the Bible

13 When Jesus came to region of Caesarea Philippi, He asked His disciples, "Who do people say that the Son of Man [this is a name Jesus often used of Himself] is?" 14 And they said, "Some say John the Baptist; others, Elijah; still others, Jeremiah or one of the prophets. 15 "But you," He asked them, "who do you say that I am?" 16 Simon Peter answered, "You are the Messiah [i.e. the Christ; the anointed one], the Son of the living God." 17 And Jesus responded, "Blessed are you, Simon son of Jonah, because flesh and blood did not reveal this to you, but My Father in heaven."

LARGE-GROUP TIME: Your leader will share some key points with you. Follow along and take notes in your *Student Books.*

Lord of Everything

2. In what ways can you rob God?

Giving Expresses Faithfulness

3. How does giving to God show your faith and trust?

4. What was a steward in biblical times?

Giving Expresses Worship

5. How is giving an expression of worship?

6. How did pouring the perfume on Jesus serve as worship for the woman?

7. How are we uniquely designed to give?

Giving Expresses Trust

8. What does trust have to do with giving to God?

9. What does the topic of giving have to do with you at this point in your life?

5

SMALL-GROUP TIME: **Small-group leaders will direct your discussions. Everyone will gain more if you are open and honest in responding to questions.**

Do What? (15 MINUTES)

Group Experience: Creative Giving

1.What has been your attitude about giving to God? Check one.

- ☐ I don't have any money, so it doesn't apply to me.
- ☐ I need all I can get, more than God does.
- ☐ All that giving business is for adults who work.
- ☐ Someone else will give.
- ☐ I never thought about giving being to God and not the church.
- ☐ I love to give to God.
- ☐ Since I don't consistently have money, I want to find other ways to give to God.
- ☐ Other: ______________________________

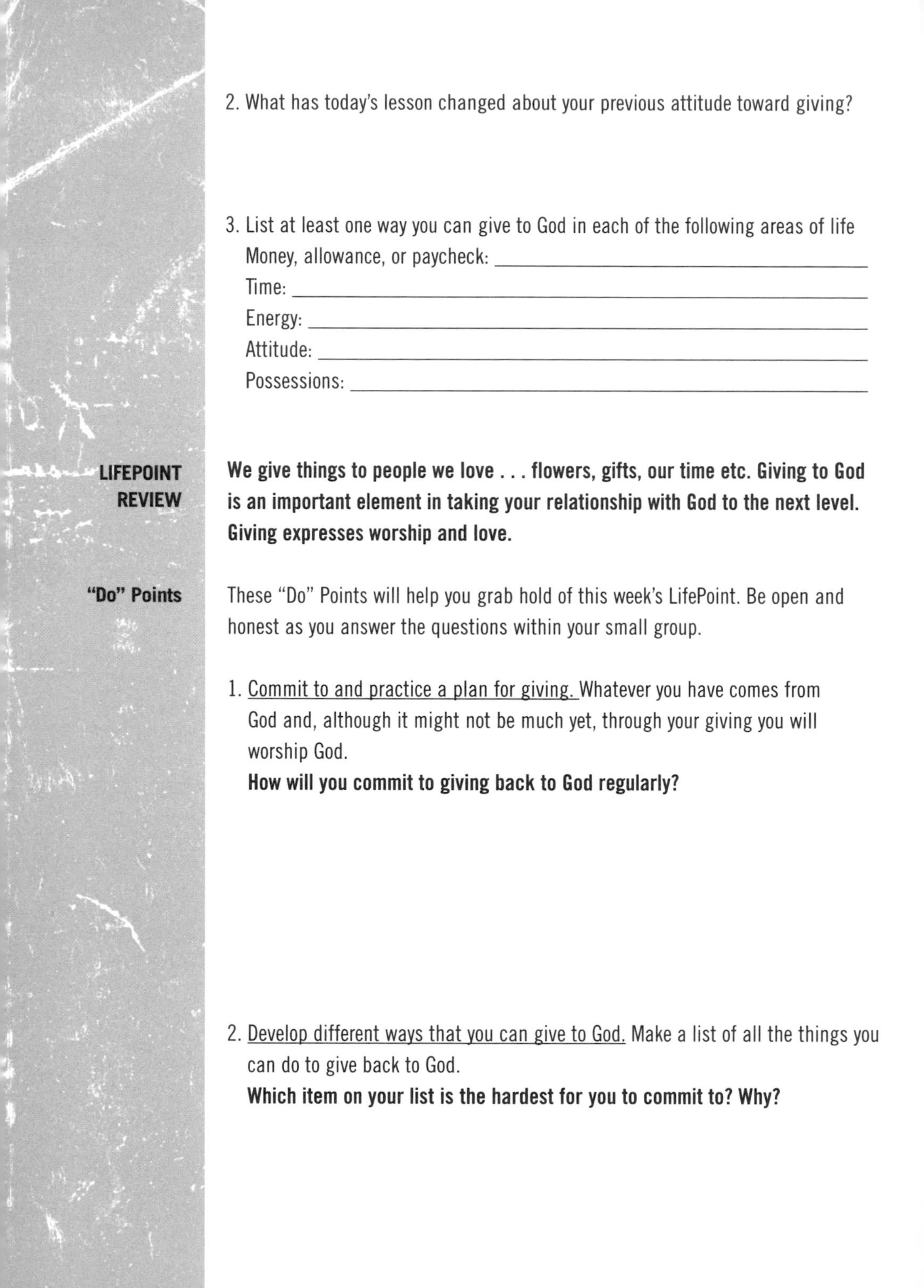

2. What has today's lesson changed about your previous attitude toward giving?

3. List at least one way you can give to God in each of the following areas of life
   Money, allowance, or paycheck: ______________________
   Time: ______________________
   Energy: ______________________
   Attitude: ______________________
   Possessions: ______________________

LIFEPOINT REVIEW

We give things to people we love . . . flowers, gifts, our time etc. Giving to God is an important element in taking your relationship with God to the next level. Giving expresses worship and love.

"Do" Points

These "Do" Points will help you grab hold of this week's LifePoint. Be open and honest as you answer the questions within your small group.

1. Commit to and practice a plan for giving. Whatever you have comes from God and, although it might not be much yet, through your giving you will worship God.
   How will you commit to giving back to God regularly?

2. Develop different ways that you can give to God. Make a list of all the things you can do to give back to God.
   Which item on your list is the hardest for you to commit to? Why?

Prayer Connection:

This is a great time to encourage and support one another in spiritual growth as you share your concerns and requests with the group.

Share prayer needs with the group, especially those that are related to hearing from God. Your group facilitator will close your time in prayer.

Prayer Needs:

Remember your "Get Ready" daily Bible readings and questions at the beginning of Session 6.

Continue on the path of spiritual growth by choosing one of the following assignments to complete this week:

Option #1:
Research the various ways that people in Scripture returned a portion God. What kinds of things did they bring Him? What were their attitudes as they gave? How were their offerings accepted? What can you learn from those examples that can help you give as worship?

Option #2:
Talk with your family about how you can commit to giving. Find out what your parents already do and offer ways to cut back on spending so that the family can be more generous with their tithes and offerings.

Bible Reference Notes

Use these notes to gain further understanding of the text as you study on your own.

Luke 12:14 ***a judge or an arbiter.*** As a rabbi, Jesus may have been asked to mediate in a dispute, in this case a family squabble. However, the request for a mediator is a thinly disguised plea for an advocate. The speaker wants Jesus to take his side. Note that this request comes as an interruption when Jesus is speaking to a crowd about persecution. Ignoring Jesus' theme and rudely disturbing Jesus' speech, the man presses his own agenda, revealing his interest in material issues rather than spiritual ones.

Luke 12:15 ***greed.*** Jesus pinpoints the real motivating factor behind this appeal for justice.
life. The Greek word here, *zoe*, refers to the quality of one's life. Then, as now, a person's happiness and well-being was often thought to be determined by what he or she owned. Jesus flatly rejects this as a standard for measuring the worth of one's life.

Luke 12:16 ***a good crop.*** In the Greek, there is a play on words as the parable develops. The man has an *euphoreo* ("good crop") which he thinks will lead to *euphron* ("the enjoyment of the good life"—v. 19), yet God calls him an *aphron* ("a fool"—v. 20).

Luke 12:19 ***eat, drink and be merry.*** It is the builder's intention to use his resources for his own self-gratification. It is a way of saying, "I can coast to the finish line from here." His declaration reveals a selfishness and a prideful sense of security.

Luke 12:20 ***your life will be demanded from you.*** The Greek text reads, "they will require of you" suggesting perhaps an angelic assignment in ending his life. In any case, it is clear that the man's life will be taken by God's directive.
who will get what you have prepared for yourself? This might be understood in two ways: (1) It points out the foolishness of living for material possessions, since at death they are of no use to the one who clung to them. He will not be the one to possess what he spent his life preparing to have! (2) It might have been intended to point out his isolation. Having chosen wealth as his god, he is alienated from friends and family. There is no one close to him to whom he can pass on an inheritance when he dies. Greed isolates people from true human relationships.

Session

6

TIME TRIAL: SPENDING A DAILY TIME WITH GOD

Get Ready

Read one of these short Bible passages each day and spend a few minutes wrapping your brain around it. Be sure to jot down any insights you discover.

MONDAY

Read Luke 10:38-39

In this passage, Mary is sitting at Jesus' feet while she listens to Him. Have you sat quietly and listened to Jesus? What was it like?

6

TUESDAY

Read Luke 10:40

Martha is distracted during her time with Jesus. What distracts you?

WEDNESDAY

Read Luke 10:41-42

What steps can you take to focus on God and ignore distractions?

THURSDAY

Read Luke 6:12-13

In this passage, Jesus spends all night praying to God. How much time do you take to pray before making decisions?

FRIDAY

Read Psalm 5:1-3

David is praying to God every morning at daybreak in this passage, and he is waiting for an answer to his prayers. What prayers are you waiting for God to answer?

SATURDAY

Read Luke 17:3-4

Who do you need to forgive as an act of faith?

SUNDAY

Read Matthew 20:25-28

Jesus came to be a servant. How are you serving others by praying for them?

LifePoint

How do you get to know someone? You spend time with him. You listen to her. And you do these things regularly. In time you will know the heart of the person. The same is true with God.

SMALL-GROUP TIME: Divide into smaller groups of 4-8, preferably in a circle. You will have a small-group leader for "Say What?"

Say What? (15 MINUTES)

Random Question of the Week:

If you could only listen to one song the rest of your life, what would it be?

Group Experience: Spend the Money

You will participate in a game led by your small-group leader.

After the game, discuss the following questions:

1. How is spending time like spending money?

2. What is one thing you regret taking time for this past week?

3. How can remembering that choosing to spend time on one thing is choosing not to spend time on something else help you make better decisions?

4. If you could have one whole day to do whatever you wanted, what would you choose to do?

G

LARGE-GROUP TIME: Turn to face the front for this teaching time. Follow along and take notes in your *Student Books.*

The Better Choice

1. What things may have distracted Martha from listening to Jesus? What distracts you?

Learning from the Bible ...

Luke 10:38-42

Learning from the Bible

38 While they were traveling, He entered a village, and a woman named Martha welcomed Him into her home. 39 She had a sister named Mary, who also sat at the Lord's feet and was listening to what He said. 40 But Martha was distracted by her many tasks, and she came up and asked, "Lord, don't You care that my sister has left me to serve alone? So tell her to give me a hand."

41 The Lord answered her, "Martha, Martha, you are worried and upset about many things, 42 but one thing is necessary. Mary has made the right choice, and it will not be taken away from her."

LARGE-GROUP TIME: Your leader will share some key points with you. Follow along and take notes in your *Student Books.*

The Purpose of Time with God

2. What is the main purpose for spending time with God daily?

3. What was Jesus' model for spending time with God?

Our Conversation

4. What is the main activity of daily time with God?

5. How can you use the Bible as the primary source through which God speaks?

6. What is the second activity of time alone with God?

7. What is a good question to ask as you read the Bible?

Developing a Balance

8. What is Jesus pointing out to us through the differences in Mary and Martha?

SMALL-GROUP TIME: Small-group leaders will direct your discussions. Everyone will gain more if you are open and honest in responding to questions.

Do What? (15 MINUTES)

1. Which one are you more like Mary or Martha? Place on X on the graph below.

o o o o o o o o o o o

Mary Martha

2. Which is the main thing that keeps you from spending time alone with God daily?
   - ☐ I need my sleep.
   - ☐ I forget.
   - ☐ It's boring to me.
   - ☐ I don't know what to do.
   - ☐ I don't have time.
   - ☐ The Bible is too hard for me to understand.
   - ☐ Other:________________________________

3. The thing that most challenged or inspired me today is

____

____

LIFEPOINT REVIEW

How do you get to know someone? You spend time with him. You listen to her. And you do these things regularly. In time you will know the heart of the person. The same is true with God.

"Do" Points

These "Do" Points will help you grab hold of this week's LifePoint. Be open and honest as you answer the questions within your small group.

1. <u>Choose a time and place to meet with God.</u> If you fail to plan, you plan to fail. **What will you do to make daily time with God a priority?**

2. Develop a plan to hear from God daily. Make hearing from God just as important as hearing from your friends. Train yourself to listen to God for a set time (like 30 seconds) and then work your way up to longer periods.
How long can you sit still and wait for God to speak?

3. Respond to what God says in an organized way. Many people keep a written journal of their responses to God.
How will you keep track of what you are asking God and what He is saying in response? (Consider a journal, blog, or webspace)

Prayer Connection:

This is the time to encourage, support, and pray for each other in our journeys to learn to hear from God.

Share prayer needs with the group, especially those that are related to hearing from God. Your group facilitator will close your time in prayer.

Prayer Needs:

Remember your "Get Ready" daily Bible readings and questions at the beginning of Session 7.

Now What?

Deepen your understanding of who God is and continue the journey you've begun today by choosing one of the following assignments to complete this week:

Option #1:
Set up an accountability group or person if you don't already have one. Challenge each other to get deeper in the Word by spending time alone with God daily. Check up on and encourage each other often. Share what you are hearing from God as you practice listening to Him.

Option #2:
Cut a piece of paper into 24 strips and designate each as an hour of the day. Divide your papers into segments and label them with whatever activity you are spending that amount of time on. Pray about the patterns that you see when you have your average day divided out. Where could you spend less time on something good so that you could switch to something better?

Bible Reference Notes

Use these notes to deepen your understanding as you study the Bible on your own:

Luke 10:38
a village. Bethany, just outside of Jerusalem (see John 11:1).
Martha. Sister of Mary and Lazarus, whom Jesus later raised from the dead.

Luke 10:39
Mary. Later we see Mary as the one who anointed Jesus with an expensive ointment while He feasted at her home in Bethany (John 12:1–8).

Luke 10:40
don't you care. Martha is not only angry with her sister Mary for not helping, but she is also accusing Jesus of being insensitive to her need for help by allowing Mary to sit at His feet instead of working in the kitchen. Note that Scripture records another of Martha's complaints against Jesus in John 11 regarding the death of Lazarus, "Lord ... if you had been here, my brother would not have died" (John 11:21). But in fairness to Martha, it should be pointed out that she immediately follows her complaint with a declaration of faith: "But I know that even now God will give you whatever you ask" (John 11:22).

Luke 10:42
but only one thing is needed. This phrase might mislead the reader to conclude that the remainder of the verse means that Mary has chosen the one thing needed, and it won't be taken away from her.
Mary has chosen what is better, and it will not be taken away from her. While Jesus is not unappreciative of Martha's hard work and hospitality, He is teaching a principle about discipleship — that spending time with God in learning and worship precedes even service.

Session

7

HEADS UP: HOW TO STUDY GOD'S WORD

Get Ready

Read one of these short Bible passages each day and spend a few minutes wrapping your brain around it. Be sure to jot down any insights you discover.

MONDAY

Read Proverbs 2:1-5

What hidden treasure have you found in the Bible?

TUESDAY

Read Proverbs 2:6

In which area of your life do you need some spiritual wisdom?

WEDNESDAY

Read 2 Timothy 3:16-17

How do you let God's Word teach, rebuke, correct, and train you?

THURSDAY

Read 2 Timothy 2:15

What steps can you take to correctly teach and represent Scripture?

FRIDAY

Read Romans 12:1-2

In what ways can the Bible renew your mind?

SATURDAY

Read Psalm 119:33-37

In what area of your life do you need more understanding?

SUNDAY

Read Psalm 143:5-6

When you think of the things God has done for you, what is the first thought that pops into your mind? Does your soul thirst for God? Why or why not?

LifePoint

The main way that you can get to know God is by studying His Word. The treasures you will find and the insight you will gain in the Bible will change your life.

SMALL-GROUP TIME: Divide into smaller groups of 4-8, preferably in a circle. You will have a small-group leader for "Say What?"

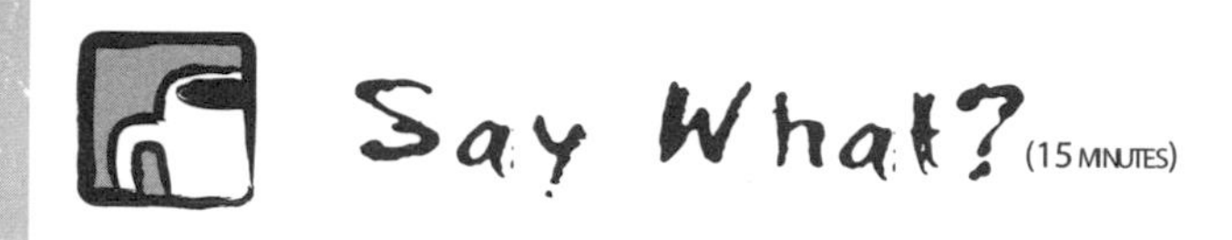

Random Question of the Week:

Where is the coldest place you have ever been?

Group Experience: National Treasure

You will watch a scene from the movie *National Treasure*.

After the clip, answer the following questions:

1. What motivated the characters to search for the clues and solve them?

2. What, if any, guarantees did they have?

3. How would it affect your search to know that there was no treasure?

4. How is a treasure hunt similar to studying the Bible?

So What? (30 MINUTES)

LARGE-GROUP TIME: Turn to face the front for this teaching time. Follow along and take notes in your *Student Books.*

A Life Long Learner

1. How long are we expected to be students of the Word?

Learning from the Bible ...

Learning from the Bible

Proverbs 2:1-6

[1] My son, if you accept my words and store up my commands within you,
[2] listening closely to wisdom and directing your heart to understanding;
[3] furthermore, if you call out to insight and lift your voice to understanding,
[4] if you seek it like silver and search for it like hidden treasure,
[5] then you will understand the fear of the Lord and discover the knowledge of God.
[6] For the Lord gives wisdom; from His mouth come knowledge and understanding.

Romans 12:1-2

[1]Therefore, brothers, by the mercies of God, I urge you to present your bodies as a living sacrifice, holy and pleasing to God; this is your spiritual worship. [2]Do not be conformed to this age, but be transformed by the renewing of your mind, so that you may discern what is the good, pleasing, and perfect will of God.

LARGE-GROUP TIME: Your leader will share some key points with you. Follow along and take notes in your *Student Books.*

A Treasure Hunt

2. What are some benefits of personal Bible study?

A Transforming Relationship

3.What are two purposes of personal Bible study?

A Study Plan

4. List two methods for studying the Bible and how they work.

5. What are the three key principles for Bible study?

6. What are some tools that you can use in your personal Bible study?

7

SMALL-GROUP TIME: Small-group leaders will direct your discussions. Everyone will gain more if you are open and honest in responding to questions.

Do What? (15 MINUTES)

Group Experience: Discovering Treasure

1. How do you think the characters felt when they saw the treasure for the first time?

2. Check the response that best describes how you feel about personal Bible study.
   - ☐ Why bother to study the Bible?
   - ☐ How can I learn anything from studying it myself?
   - ☐ I'm stressed out by it because I don't know how to do it!
   - ☐ It is one of my favorite times of the day.
   - ☐ Other: ______________________________

3. Will the loved ones you leave behind have any cause to doubt where you will spend eternity? Why or why not?

4. Think of one "treasure" you have gotten from the Bible. Share your treasure with the group. If you can't think of a treasure, write one treasure you would like to find.

LIFEPOINT REVIEW

The main way that you can get to know God is by studying His Word. The treasures you will find and the insight you will gain in the Bible will change your life forever.

"Do" Points

These "Do" Points will help you grab hold of this week's LifePoint. Be open and honest as you answer the questions within your small group.

1. Study God's Word like a journalist. Journalists ask questions like Who? What? Where? When? How? Why?
   Does your life reflect your belief in eternity? Explain.

2. Study God's Word like a detective. Detectives look for clues to solve mysteries.
   How is the Bible like a mystery?

3. Study God's Word like an athlete. A great athlete will train, research, practice, and then apply what he or she has accomplished through these disciplines.
   How can you apply your knowledge of the things you are learning to your life this week?

7

Prayer Connection:

This is the time to encourage, support, and pray for each other. Share prayer needs with the group, especially those related to trusting in the hope of eternity through Jesus—even on days when everything seems to be going wrong. Your group facilitator will close your time in prayer.

Prayer Needs:

Remember your "Get Ready" daily Bible readings and questions at the beginning of Session 8.

Deepen your understanding of who God is and continue the journey you've begun today by choosing one of the following assignments to complete this week:

Option #1:
Choose a short book of the Bible or a chapter from a book of the Bible that interests you and read a few verses at a time. In a journal, log some questions you might have. Ask questions as an athlete, a detective, or a journalist might. Once done, use some of the tools that we've mentioned to find answers to your questions. Enter these answers in your journal.

Option #2:
Conduct some online research to find places where you can get study tools and helps for understanding Scripture. Bring the results of your search you see as most helpful to the next meeting and share them with the group.

Bible Reference Notes

Use these notes to deepen your understanding as you study the Bible on your own:

Proverbs 2:1

accept my words. Solomon declares a hope that his son will trust his teaching. Key idea: Attention.
store up my commands within you. This is the hope that his son will value his teaching, keep it, protect it, and remember it. A contemporary paraphrase might be, "I hope that you won't throw away this teaching or just toss it in a file folder somewhere but will value it and keep it close at hand where you can see and think about it." Key idea: Retention.

11:44 bound hand and foot with linen strips. While burial customs included wrapping the body with cloth and spices (19:40), this was not intended to preserve the body, like the ancient Egyptian process of mummification. It only served as a sign of honor for the deceased person.

Proverbs 2:2

turning your ear to wisdom. Choose to listen to wise instruction. Contrast to 2 Timothy 4:3–5. Key idea: Selection.
applying your heart to understanding. Dedicating yourself to the labor of understanding, not just listening. Key idea: Reflection.

Proverbs 2:3

call out for insight and cry aloud for understanding. Wisdom must be craved and pursued (see James 1:5).

Proverbs 2:4

look for it as for silver ... as for hidden treasure. Neither silver nor hidden treasure is found on the surface. Both must be dug out. As in verse 3, the emphasis is upon desire and effort.

Proverbs 2:5

the fear of the Lord. In Proverbs 1:7, Solomon declares that "The fear of the Lord is the beginning of knowledge." Fear of the Lord begins with knowing Him. Closely linked is a reverence for God, expressed in the acknowledgment of His holiness and power and demonstrated in the submission to His will. This acknowledgment of the supreme authority of God is the foundation to wise thinking and right living.

Proverbs 2:6

the Lord gives wisdom. God, having all knowledge, is completely wise and correct in all matters. Furthermore, God delights in imparting His wisdom to those who would welcome it (see James 1:5). God was greatly pleased that of all the gifts and blessings offered to Him, Solomon requested divinely enabled wisdom (2 Chron. 1:7–12; 2:12).

NOTES

Session

FILL UP: MEDITATING AND MEMORIZING GOD'S WORD

Get Ready

Read one of these short Bible passages each day and spend a few minutes wrapping your brain around it. Be sure to jot down any insights you discover.

MONDAY

Read Psalm 119:97

David loves God's teaching, so he meditates on it. What does it mean to meditate on a Scripture passage?

TUESDAY

Read Psalm 119:98

David says God's commands make him smarter than his enemies. How do God's commands make you wiser?

WEDNESDAY

Read Psalm 119:99-100

David says he is wiser than his teachers and his elders because he meditates on God's teachings and obeys them. How can meditation help you understand more?

THURSDAY

Read Psalm 119:101-102

Describe a time when you, like David, felt as if God was teaching you Himself?

FRIDAY

Read Psalm 119:11-16

David treasures God's Word, and it keeps him from sin. How has the Bible helped you during times of temptation?

SATURDAY

Read 1 Peter 3:15-16

Peter says we must know the Bible well enough to explain our faith at any time using Scriptures. How could you use Scripture to defend your faith?

SUNDAY

Read Proverbs 22:17-18

Why is it important to keep Scripture constantly on your lips?

LifePoint

We must allow the Holy Spirit to work in our lives through Scripture in order to become the people we have been created to be. The best way to get the Word of God into your heart and mind is to meditate on it and memorize it.

SMALL-GROUP TIME: Divide into smaller groups of 4-8, preferably in a circle. You will have a small-group leader for "Say What?"

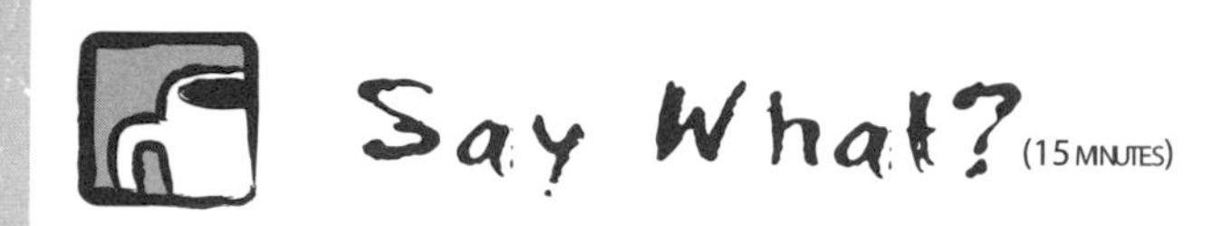

Random Question of the Week:

What is your earliest childhood memory?

Group Experience: Fill in the Blank

You will participate in an experiment led by your small-group leader.

After the experiment, discuss the following questions:

1. How would you rate your ability to memorize? Place an X on the graph below.

○ ○ ○ ○ ○ ○ ○ ○ ○ ○ ○

I can barely remember my own name — I have a photographic memory

2. What are the easiest things for you to memorize? Check all that apply.
   - ☐ Songs
   - ☐ Music
   - ☐ Quotes
   - ☐ Ad jingles
   - ☐ Algebraic equations
   - ☐ Video game answers
   - ☐ Phone numbers
   - ☐ Scripture
   - ☐ Other: ____________________

3. What makes some things easier to memorize than others?

8

LARGE-GROUP TIME: Turn to face the front for this teaching time. Follow along and take notes in your *Student Books.*

So What? (30 MINUTES)

Meditate and Memorize

1. Why does the mention of meditation and memorization elicit a negative response from many Christians?

Learning from the Bible ...

Psalm 119:97-102

Learning from the Bible

97 How I love Your teaching!
It is my meditation all day long.
98 Your command makes me wiser than my enemies,
for it is always with me.
99 I have more insight than all my teachers
because Your decrees are my meditation.
100 I understand more than the elders
because I obey Your precepts.
101 I have kept my feet from every evil path
to follow Your word.
102 I have not turned from Your judgments,
for You Yourself have instructed me.

LARGE-GROUP TIME: Your leader will share some key points with you. Follow along and take notes in your *Student Books.*

Meditation Misconceptions

2. What are some common misconceptions about Christian meditation?

The Practice of Meditation

3. What benefits does Scripture meditation provide?

4. Give two ways to meditate using Scripture.

Commit it to Memory

5. List the four benefits to memorizing Scripture from today's lesson:
   1.helps me resist ____________________
   2.helps me make ____________________
   3.it ________ and ____________________ me when I have trouble
   4.it helps me encourage others and ________________ to unbelievers

SMALL-GROUP TIME: Small-group leaders will direct your discussions. Everyone will gain more if you are open and honest in responding to questions.

Do What? (15 MINUTES)

Group Experience: It Takes Time

1. What did you learn about Christian meditation from the tea bag example?

2. How much of your life is currently absorbed by the Word of God?
   - ☐ Slightly absorbed
   - ☐ None at all
   - ☐ Completely absorbed
   - ☐ Still absorbing
   - ☐ Other: ____________________

8

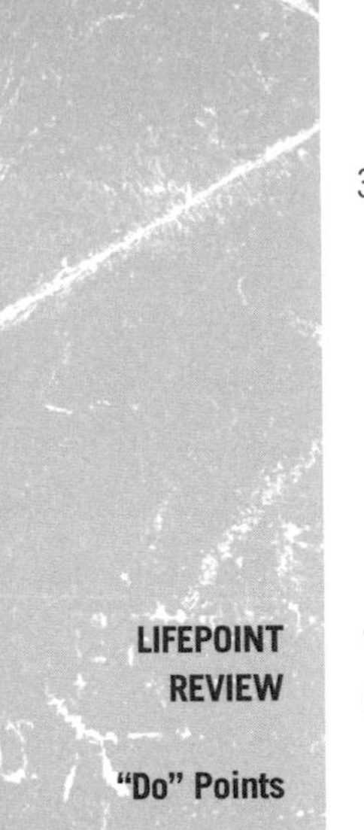

3. How will today's lesson change your life?

LIFEPOINT REVIEW

We must allow the Holy Spirit to work in our lives through Scripture in order to become the people we have been created to be. The best way to get the Word of God into your heart and mind is to meditate on it and memorize it.

"Do" Points

These "Do" Points will help you grab hold of this week's LifePoint. Be open and honest as you answer the questions within your small group.

1. Practice the five methods of Scripture meditation this week. Look at the methods below and try them out.
   Which method do you think will be most effective for you?
   - ☐ Meditation
   - ☐ Picture it-visualize the scene in your mind
   - ☐ Pronounce it-say the verse aloud emphasizing a different word each time
   - ☐ Paraphrase it-rewrite the verse in your own words
   - ☐ Personalize it-put your own name into the verse
   - ☐ Pray it-turn the verse into a prayer and say it back to God

2. Memorize 1 or 2 new Scripture verses this week using the 10 strategies.
   1. Choose a verse that is meaningful to you
   2. Say the reference before and after the verse
   3. Read the verse aloud many times
   4. Break longer verses in to thoughts
   5. Emphasize key words when quoting the verse
   6. Write the verse on an index card
   7. Carry the cards with you and review them daily
   8. Keep the verses where you can read them often
   9. Put the verse to music and sing it
   10. Find a formal memorization system to use

   Which verse will you memorize first?

Prayer Connection:

This is the time to encourage, support, and pray for each other in our journeys to learn to hear from God.

Share prayer needs with the group, especially those that are related to hearing from God. Your group facilitator will close your time in prayer.

Prayer Needs:

Remember your "Get Ready" daily Bible readings and questions at the beginning of Session 9

Continue on the path of spiritual growth by choosing one of the following assignments to complete this week:

Option #1:
Spend a set time each day meditating on a Scripture verse or passage. Keep a journal of what you learn from these times.

Option #2:
Research meditation and memorization by looking them up in a concordance. Make a list all the things you learn about these two practices of spiritual disciplines.

Bible Reference Notes

Use these notes to gain further understanding of the text as you study on your own.

Psalm 119:97

law. The law is the moral and ethical teachings of the Old Testament. While the psalmist had only the Old Testament law, the Christian has the "perfect law that gives freedom" (James 1:25).

Psalm 119:99

statutes. A statute or decree is akin to a legal and binding policy, a law.

Psalm 119:100

the elders. The Hebrew word for elder means literally "bearded ones," perhaps a commentary on age, experience, and wisdom. Their duties included acting as judges in legal matters and leaders in military matters.
obey your precepts. A precept is a guideline for conduct, a principle for life.

Psalm 119:102

you yourself have taught me. While the psalmist certainly profited from educated and godly teachers, he did not rely merely on hearing or studying their interpretations. He also studied the Word himself, allowing the Spirit of God to be his teacher.

Session

9

WORD UP: APPLYING GOD'S WORD TO MY LIFE

Get Ready

Read one of these short Bible passages each day and spend a few minutes wrapping your brain around it. Be sure to jot down any insights you discover.

MONDAY

Read Matthew 7:24-27

In this parable, Jesus explains that we must build on rock, not on sand. What characteristics would you expect to find in a solid foundation? How many of these are present in your life?

TUESDAY

Read James 1:22

Would say that you are a "hearer" or a "doer" of God's Word? Why?

9

WEDNESDAY

Read James 1:23-25

According to this passage, doers of the Word will be blessed. When have you walked away from a conviction and "forgotten" to do what God has asked?

THURSDAY

Read Matthew 5:21-26

How easily do you get angry? In what ways are you unforgiving toward fellow believers?

FRIDAY

Read Matthew 5:33-37

How well are others able to trust you and your word?

SATURDAY

Read Matthew 6:25-33

Jesus teaches in this work that we should not worry about tomorrow, because tomorrow will worry about itself. In what ways is your faith bigger than all your worries?

SUNDAY

Read Romans 12:9-13

Of all the things listed in this passage, which is God asking you to do today?

LifePoint

Hearing the truth is the starting point, but simply hearing truth doesn't bring change. You must apply God's Word to your life.

SMALL-GROUP TIME: Divide into smaller groups of 4-8, preferably in a circle. You will have a small-group leader for "Say What?"

Say What? (15 MINUTES)

Random Question of the Week:

What is your favorite children's story?

Group Experience: The Three Pigs

You will listen to a story read by your small-group leader.

After the story, discuss the following questions:

1. What lesson can you learn from *The Three Little Pigs*?

2. Which of the little pigs are you most like? How?

3. Rank the following in order of importance to you. 1 will be least important and 7 will be most important.
    1._______Happiness
    2._______Wisdom
    3._______Joy
    4. ______Money
    5. ______Good looks
    6._______Big house
    7._______Cool jeans

Where does wisdom rank on your list of things you desire?

9

LARGE-GROUP TIME: Turn to face the front for this teaching time. Follow along and take notes in your *Student Books.*

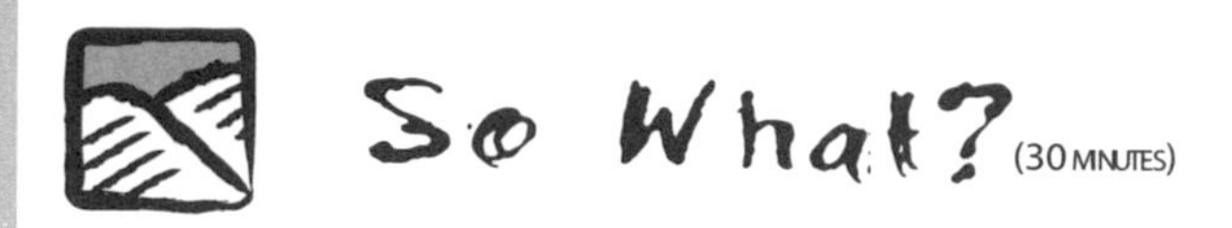

The Power of Obedience

1. What are the two types of builders that Jesus contrasted in Matthew 7?

Learning from the Bible ...

Matthew 7:24-27 and James 1:22-25

Learning from the Bible

[24] "Therefore, everyone who hears these words of Mine and acts on them will be like a sensible man who built his house on the rock. [25] The rain fell, the rivers rose, and the winds blew and pounded that house. Yet it didn't collapse, because its foundation was on the rock. [26] But everyone who hears these words of Mine and doesn't act on them will be like a foolish man who built his house on the sand. [27] The rain fell, the rivers rose, the winds blew and pounded that house, and it collapsed. And its collapse was great!"

Matthew 7:24-27

LARGE-GROUP TIME: Your leader will share some key points with you. Follow along and take notes in your *Student Books.*

[22] But be doers of the word and not hearers only, deceiving yourselves. [23] Because if anyone is a hearer of the word and not a doer, he is like a man looking at his own face in a mirror; [24] for he looks at himself, goes away, and right away forgets what kind of man he was. [25] But the one who looks intently into the perfect law of freedom and perseveres in it, and is not a forgetful hearer but a doer who acts—this person will be blessed in what he does.

James 1:22-25

The Purpose of Scripture

2. What are the two main purposes of Scripture?

Applying the Word to Life

3. Hearing the truth is a place to start.

4. What types of people are being contrasted in Matthew 7:24-27?

5. The steps toward application are:
    A. __________not just exposure
    B. __________not just occasionally
    C. __________not just storing
    D. __________not burdens

SMALL-GROUP TIME: Small-group leaders will direct your discussions. Everyone will gain more if you are open and honest in responding to questions.

Do What? (15 MINUTES)

Out to Impress?

1. What has God revealed to you that you have failed to apply?

2. Choose your favorite analogy from the list. Share how you can use it this week to remind you about the importance of applying God's Word to your life.
   - ☐ Getting dressed up with no place to go
   - ☐ Collecting brochures that promote great places but never traveling
   - ☐ Reading books on weight training but never lifting a weight
   - ☐ Practice, train, and study but never compete
   - ☐ Being a West Point graduate and only playing with GI Joe figures
   - ☐ Getting a medical degree and working in a coffee shop

3. Share about a time when you knew what Scripture had to say about a specific circumstance yet failed to apply it. Were there any consequences?

4. Which of the four "Steps toward Application" was most challenging to you? Why?
   - ☐ Examination, not just exposure
   - ☐ Consistently, not just occasionally
   - ☐ Activating, not just storing
   - ☐ Blessings, not just burdens

LIFEPOINT REVIEW

"Do" Points

Hearing the truth is the starting point, but simply hearing truth doesn't bring change. You must apply God's Word to your life.

These "Do" Points will help you grab hold of this week's LifePoint. Be open and honest as you answer the questions within your small group.

1. 1. Ask the S.P.A.C.E.P.E.T.S. questions when reading Scripture. Is there any . . .
   · **S**in to confess?
   · **P**romise to claim?
   · **A**ttitude to change?
   · **C**ommand to obey?
   · **E**xample to follow?
   · **P**rayer to pray?
   · **E**rror to avoid?
   · **T**ruth to believe?
   · **S**omething to thank/praise God for?
   How can you become familiar with these questions and put them to regular use?

2. Identify one or two of your most urgent responses from your S.P.A.C.E.P.E.T.S. answers. You can't work on too many things at one time.
   Which of the S.P.A.C.E.P.E.T.S. questions are most helpful to you?
   How can you use them to apply the Word?

Prayer Connection:

This is the time to encourage, support, and pray for each other in our journeys to learn to hear from God.

Share prayer needs with the group, especially those that are related to hearing from God. Your group facilitator will close your time in prayer.

Prayer Needs:

Remember your "Get Ready" daily Bible readings and questions at the beginning of Session 10.

Continue on the path of spiritual growth by choosing one of the following assignments to complete this week:

Option #1:
Make personal application as practical as possible by asking the Journalist Questions. These questions can help you identify what God is saying to you through a particular passage.

- What do I need to know about this matter?
- Who does this involve?
- When do I need to take action?
- Where do I need to apply this?
- Why should I take this action?
- How should I proceed?

Using the Journalist Questions, develop a plan of action to begin applying Scripture to your life.

Option #2:
Do a foundation study in the Bible as you look up references to foundations. Then, examine your life to identify what you are building on. Looks? Grades? Family? Popularity? How are these things just like the sand that the foolish man built his house on?

Bible Reference Notes

Use these notes to gain further understanding of the text as you study on your own.

Matthew 7:24

built his house on the rock. This does not suggest that the house was built on the surface of a rock but that its foundation (see v. 25b) was set deeply into firm, rocky soil.

Matthew 7:25

rain came down, the streams rose, and the winds blew. There is no need to analyze separately the symbolism of the rain, river, and wind as it is simply an accumulative metaphor for life's inevitable problems, crises, and pressures that will judge the quality of construction. For example, Hurricane Andrew exposed inferior construction as it tore through Homestead, Florida.

Matthew 7:26

foolish man who built his house on sand. Since rushing water would easily erode the loose sand surrounding an insecure foundation, the entire structure was vulnerable to being washed away or collapsing upon itself. The foolish builder thinks only of the present while the wise builder considers the future and solid construction.

James 1:22

and so deceive yourselves. Don't be deceived into thinking that merely hearing the Word is sufficient and earns special favor with God. In fact, there is a greater responsibility and accountability placed upon those who have heard than those who have not heard. If hearing is not combined with action, they may put themselves in as vulnerable a position as the foolish man described in Matthew 7:26–27.
looks at his face in a mirror ... and immediately forgets what he looks like. The mirror gives feedback that can be used to make adjustments or corrections (see 2 Tim. 3:16–17). The Greek verb *katanoeo* does not imply a hasty glance as some suggest. Rather, it denotes careful observation. The man carefully studies his face and has complete knowledge of its features, just as a man who carefully hears, reads, and studies the Scripture then has full understanding of the teaching and is accountable for his knowledge.

James 1:25

looks intently. The Greek word is *parakypto.* It is the same word used to describe John's act of stooping and peering into Jesus' tomb (John 20:5). Thus, the wise man stoops for a close, thorough examination of the Scripture.
the perfect law. The moral and ethical teachings of Christianity (see Ps. 19:7).
that gives freedom. Obeying the Word of God liberates us from being a slave to sin (see John 8:34; Rom. 6:6; Gal. 4:7). James is also using irony in that the Law is usually seen as restricting behavior. James, however, insists that the Law perfected by Jesus (see Matt. 5:17) gives freedom (see Matt. 11:28–30; 23:1–4.)
he will be blessed in what he does. There will be positive results for active obedience as opposed to negative consequences for delay or disobedience (see Gal. 6:7–9).

NOTES

Session

10

GAME ON: LIVING IN THE POWER OF THE SPIRIT

Get Ready

Read one of these short Bible passages each day and spend a few minutes wrapping your brain around it. Be sure to jot down any insights you discover.

MONDAY

Read Galatians 5:16

This verse tells us that we won't carry out the desires of the flesh if we are walking in the power of the Holy Spirit. What makes living a Spirit-led life difficult?

TUESDAY

Read Galatians 5:17

The Spirit and our flesh are in opposition to each other so that we don't do what we want to do. How often do you do things you know you shouldn't?

WEDNESDAY

Read Galatians 5:18-21

We are told in these verses that the works of the flesh are obvious. With which of these acts of the sinful nature listed in this passage do you struggle?

THURSDAY

Read Galatians 5:22-23

Which of the fruits of the Spirit listed in this passage do you see in your life? Which would you like to see more often?

FRIDAY

Read Galatians 5:24-25

We learn that those who belong to Christ have crucified the flesh. What distracts you the most when it comes to hearing the Holy Spirit?

SATURDAY

Read Romans 8:26-27

What does it mean to you that the Holy Spirit intercedes for you and helps you in your weakness?

SUNDAY

Read Ephesians 5:15-18

This passage tells us to pay careful attention to how we walk because the days are evil. What does "the days are evil" mean to you? How careful are you about the way you live?

LifePoint

Scripture encourages us to walk in the Spirit. Walking in the Spirit means walking in a spiritual manner throughout all the moments and activities of our daily routines.

SMALL-GROUP TIME: Divide into maller groups of -8, preferably in circle. You will have a small-group leader for "Say What?"

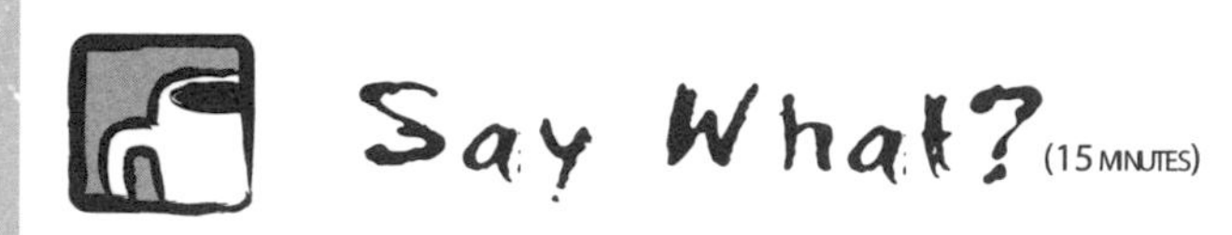

Random Question of the Week:

If you only cut people's hair that refuse to cut it themselves, would you cut your own hair?

Group Experience: Walk On

For each pair below, choose which type of walking you would rather do.

- ☐ Walk in fresh snow
- ☐ Walk on the beach

- ☐ Hike a mountain trail
- ☐ Walk in a shopping mall

- ☐ Walk in a political rally
- ☐ Walk in a charity walkathon

- ☐ Tour the Smithsonian
- ☐ Cover Disney World

- ☐ Walk through Hershey's chocolate factory
- ☐ Tour a BMW plant

- ☐ Walk across the Golden Gate Bridge
- ☐ Walk across a rope bridge over the Colorado River

- ☐ Walk to an ice cream shop
- ☐ Walk to Starbucks

- ☐ Walk to the top of the Statue of Liberty
- ☐ Walk down into the Grand Canyon

After the activity, give a piece of candy to everyone still standing, and then discuss the following questions:

1. What do your choices say about you?

2. Throughout Scripture, walking is compared with how we live our lives. Which of the following is most true about you right now?
 - ☐ I walk alone.
 - ☐ I walk in front.
 - ☐ I only walk in a crowd. Wherever they go is fine by me.
 - ☐ I like to follow the right person.
 - ☐ I am picky about who I walk with.
 - ☐ I never walk unless it's from the couch to the fridge.
 - ☐ Other: ______________________________

LARGE-GROUP TIME: Turn to face the front for this teaching time. Follow along and take notes in your *Student Books.*

So What? (30 MINUTES)

Power Walking

1. In the Bible, walking is a metaphor used to describe _________ ________.

Learning from the Bible ...

Galatians 5:16-25

Learning from the Bible

[16] I say then, walk by the Spirit and you will not carry out the desire of the flesh. [17] For the flesh desires what is against the Spirit, and the Spirit desires what is against the flesh; these are opposed to each other, so that you don't do what you want. [18] But if you are led by the Spirit, you are not under the law.

LARGE-GROUP TIME: Your leader will share some key points with you. Follow along and take notes in your *Student Books.*

[19] Now the works of the flesh are obvious: sexual immorality, moral impurity, promiscuity, [20] idolatry, sorcery, hatreds, strife, jealousy, outbursts of anger, selfish ambitions, dissensions, factions, [21] envy, drunkenness, carousing, and anything similar, about which I tell you in advance—as I told you before—that those who practice such things will not inherit the kingdom of God.

[22] But the fruit of the Spirit is love, joy, peace, patience, kindness, goodness, faith, [23] gentleness, self-control. Against such things there is no law. [24] Now those who belong to Christ Jesus have crucified the flesh with its passions and desires. [25] If we live by the Spirit, we must also follow the Spirit.

Warm Up – Understanding the Holy Spirit's Role

2. What are the 3 indicators that the Holy Spirit is a person and not a force?
   A.
   B.
   C.

3. Fill in the blanks of these truths about the Holy Spirit.
   A. He guides into ____________________
   B. He convicts us of ____________________
   C. He performs ____________________
   D. He is to be ____________________
   E. He can be ______________ to ______________
   F. He can be ____________________
   G. He ______________for us ______________
   H. He can be ____________________
   I. He gives ____________________

Do the Walk – Engage the Holy Spirit's Power

4. Describe the process of "spiritual breathing".

5. What is the opposite of being filled with the Holy Spirit?

6. What does it mean to be under the influence of the Holy Spirit?

7. What is the evidence of being filled with the Holy Spirit?

Do What? (15 MINUTES)

SMALL-GROUP TIME: Small-group leaders will direct your discussions. Everyone will gain more if you are open and honest in responding to questions.

Group Experience: The Unlit Bulb

1. What did the light bulb illustration reveal to you?

2. If you are the bulb, which best describes you today?
   - ☐ I'm still in the package.
   - ☐ I'm plugged in to the wrong power source.
   - ☐ I'm burned out.
   - ☐ I'm forgotten in a box of decorations.
   - ☐ I'm plugged in and shining bright.
   - ☐ Other: ____________________________

3. What did you learn today about the Holy Spirit that surprised you?

LIFEPOINT REVIEW

Scripture encourages us to walk in the Spirit. Walking in the Spirit means walking in a spiritual manner throughout all the moments and activities of our daily routines.

"Do" Points

These "Do" Points will help you grab hold of this week's LifePoint. Be open and honest as you answer the questions within your small group.

1. <u>Seek the Holy Spirit's filling each day.</u> This should be a continual thing—not a one-time event.
   Why should you begin each day with a refilling of the Holy Spirit?

2. <u>Practice spiritual breathing throughout the day.</u> Spiritual breathing is the process of exhaling the negative (confessing any sins which are hindering the work of the Spirit in your life) and inhaling the Spirit (accepting His filling by faith).
   How can spiritual breathing change the way you live your life?

3. Reflect on the day at bedtime. We learn from reflecting on our experiences, and if you are in too big of a hurry to reflect, then you may miss seeing ways that you can live better in the power of the Holy Spirit.
Will you commit to taking the time to reflect and pray at the end of each day so that you can ask the Spirit to show you where you fell short?

Prayer Connection:

This is the time to encourage, support, and pray for each other in our journeys to learn to hear from God.

Share prayer needs with the group, especially those that are related to hearing from God. Your group facilitator will close your time in prayer.

Prayer Needs:

Remember your "Get Ready" daily Bible readings and questions at the beginning of Session 11.

Now What?

Go a little deeper with God in your spiritual journey by completing one of these assignments this week.

Option #1:

Make a list of all the things that fill your life. Where does the Holy Spirit fit? Pray and ask God to show you the areas of your life that you need to release to His control and confess those. Then, ask the Holy Spirit to fill you and be the one who takes control.

Option #2:

Research more about the Holy Spirit and all He does. Look Him up in a concordance and read verses that are written specifically about Him and His characteristics. Keep a list of your findings. Make notes about the way that you have experienced His power.

Bible Reference Notes

Use these notes to deepen your understanding as you study the Bible on your own:

Galatians 5:16

live by the Spirit. This verb tense translates as "go on living," speaking of habitual conduct. Live continuously, moment-by-moment, by the promptings and power of the Holy Spirit.
the sinful nature. At the moment a sinner trusts Christ for salvation, his identity and eternal destiny is immediately transformed. His old ways of behavior, however, are well-conditioned and resistant to submission to the will and character of God.

Galatians 5:16

you do not do what you want. The sinful nature keeps you from doing the good that you desire to do (Rom. 7:15–16).

Galatians 5:18

led by the Spirit. See Romans 8:13–14.
you are not under law. Not under the bondage of trying to earn God's approval through keeping a seemingly endless list of laws and rules for salvation and sanctification.

Galatians 5:19-21

Paul divides the acts of the sinful nature (or the works of the flesh) into four areas: sexual sins, spiritual sins, social sins, and drinking sins. Note that listing vices and virtues was standard practice among moral teachers, including biblical writers (1 Cor. 13:4–7; 2 Cor. 6:1–10, 8:1–7; Eph. 4:1–10; Phil. 4:8–9; Col. 3:12–17; 1 Tim. 6:6–8; 2 Tim. 3:2–4; 2 Peter 1:5–8). The lists are not a legal checklist and neither are they meant to be exhaustive. The lists are context specific. That is, the lists take into consideration some special issue or need among the people to whom they were written.

Galatians 5:19

sexual immorality, impurity and debauchery. (sexual sins) Sexual immorality = sexual behavior between unmarrieds or adultery among marrieds; impurity = unnatural vice such as homosexuality; debauchery = open, reckless, unashamed contempt of propriety.

Galatians 5:20

idolatry and witchcraft. (spiritual sins) Idolatry = anything apart from God receiving worship; witchcraft = engaging the powers of evil.
hatred, discord, jealousy, fits of rage, selfish ambition, dissensions, factions, and envy. (social sins) This area appears to be Paul's focus given that it has considerably more detail than the others. Look at the verses (Gal. 5:15,26) which sandwich the focal passage of the session. (The social sins are not defined since they are rather clear.)
drunkenness, orgies, and the like. (drinking sins) Drunkenness = the state of drunkenness and corresponding behaviors; orgies = degenerate and unrestrained behavior.

Galatians 5:21

those who live like this. The Greek verb *prasso* implies habitual practice, not occasional doing, *poieo.*
will not inherit the kingdom of God. The habit of these sins is proof that a person is not in the kingdom of God and will not inherit it.

Galatians 5:22-23

the fruit of the Spirit. In contrast to the acts of the sinful nature, or works of the flesh, the use of "fruit" implies a certain sense of passivity, emphasizing that it is a divine enabling that produces these qualities. As someone has said, "If you listen closely you will not hear an orange tree grunting trying to produce oranges. The life flowing through the tree produces the fruit." Consider the parallel principle of abiding in Jesus found in John 15:5.
the fruit of the Spirit is love, joy, peace, patience, kindness, goodness, faithfulness, gentleness and self-control. While these words are filled with meaning, the terms are relatively clear and are thus not defined or described in further detail here.
Against such things there is no law. An understatement used for rhetorical effect. While the Law was given to restrain evil, the behaviors reflected in the fruit of the Spirit need no restraint.

Galatians 5:24

crucified the sinful nature. We act based on the fact that our flesh (sinful nature) has been placed on the cross and crucified with Christ (Rom. 6:11; Gal. 2:20).

Galatians 5:25

keep in step with the Spirit. Or "walk in line with the Holy Spirit." The Spirit leads and we are to follow.

NOTES

Session

11

POWER UP: RESISTING TEMPTATION

Get Ready

Read one of these short Bible passages each day and spend a few minutes wrapping your brain around it. Be sure to jot down any insights you discover.

MONDAY

Read James 1:2-4

James explains in these verses how the testing of our faith produces endurance. How can testing your faith produce endurance?

TUESDAY

Read James 1:12

James insinuates that we are taking a test when we endure trials. What was your most recent "test"? What grade would you give yourself? Why?

WEDNESDAY

Read James 1:13-15

This passage explains that God never tempts us. Who does? How? (Look at verse 14.)

THURSDAY

Read 1 John 2:15-17

Which of these elements—the lust of the flesh, the lust of the eyes, or pride in your lifestyle—gives you the biggest problem?

FRIDAY

Read 1 Peter 5:8-11

How can you best stand guard against Satan? How can you resist your greatest enemy? What does this passage say God will personally for us after we have suffered a little?

SATURDAY

Read 1 Corinthians 10:13

How has God provided a means of escape from temptation for you?

SUNDAY

Read Psalm 119:11

The psalmist is describing how Scripture has helped not to sin. Has Scripture ever come to mind when you were tempted, afraid, or worried? What action can you take to ensure that Scripture comes to your mind more often?

LifePoint

You have an enemy, and his main purpose is to destroy you in order to cause injury to God. However, because of Jesus' sacrifice, we can have victory over temptation and freedom from its entanglements.

SMALL-GROUP TIME: Divide into smaller groups of 4–8, preferably in a circle. You will have a small-group leader for "Say What?"

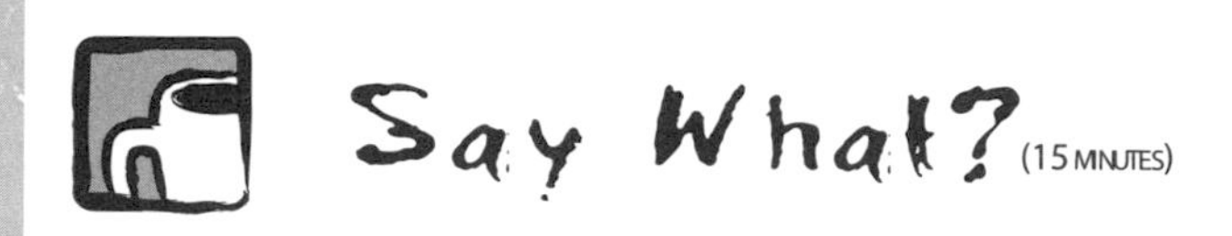

Random Question of the Week:

If you could compete in any Olympic event, which event would you choose?

Group Experience: Cool Running

You will watch a scene from the movie *Cool Running*.

After you watch the clip, discuss the following questions:

1. What part of the clip had the most impact on you?

2. Would the coach have made the same choice had he known the consequences of his decision to cheat? Why or why not?

3. How does considering the consequences help you resist temptation? What we do while here on earth?

LARGE-GROUP TIME: Turn to face the front for this teaching time. Follow along and take notes in your *Student Books.*

Temptation

1. Simply put, ___________is a part of our reality and _______ _______ _____

Learning from the Bible ...

James 1:12-15 (NASB)

Learning from the Bible

[12] Blessed is a man who perseveres under trial; for once he has been approved, he will receive the crown of life which the Lord has promised to those who love Him. [13] Let no one say when he is tempted, "I am being tempted by God"; for God cannot be tempted by evil, and He Himself does not tempt anyone. [14] But each one is tempted when he is carried away and enticed by his own lust. [15] Then when lust has conceived, it gives birth to sin; and when sin is accomplished, it brings forth death.

LARGE-GROUP TIME: Your leader will share some key points with you. Follow along and take notes in your *Student Books.*

The Difference Between Tests and Temptations

2. What is the difference between testing and temptation?

The Benefits of Tests and Temptations

3. What are the benefits of testing?

4. What is a possible result of resisting temptation?

Three Sources of Temptation

5. What are the three sources of temptation?

6. Name three channels through which temptation comes through our physical world.

7. How does the flesh contribute to temptation?

Three Root Sins

8. What are the three root sins?

The Sequence of Temptation

9. Identify the 7 steps of temptation found in James 1:14-15.

1. The ______________________________ - he is dragged away
2. The ______________________________ - by his own evil desire
3. The ______________________________- and enticed
4. The ______________________________ - then, after desire has conceived
5. The ______________________________ - it gives birth to sin
6. The ______________________________ - and sin when it is full-grown
7. The ______________________________ - gives birth to death

SMALL-GROUP TIME: **Small-group leaders will direct your discussions. Everyone will gain more if you are open and honest in responding to questions.**

Do What? (15 MINUTES)

Group Experience: The Strongest Animal

1. How do you think the stuffed animal illustration relates to today's lesson?

2. Today, which animal is stronger in your life? Flesh or spirit? Why?

3. List three or four ways that you can strengthen the spiritual nature in yourself so that it will win the battles with your flesh.

LIFEPOINT REVIEW

You have an enemy, and his main purpose is to destroy you in order to cause injury to God. However, because of Jesus' sacrifice, we can have victory over temptation and freedom from its entanglements.

"Do" Points

These "Do" Points will help you grab hold of this week's LifePoint. Risk being open and honest as you answer the questions within your small group.

1. <u>Use Scripture as a weapon to resist temptation.</u> There is power in the Word. **How can you be more prepared to use Scripture as a weapon?**

2. <u>Learn to starve sin.</u> If something isn't fed, it won't grow and will eventually die. **How can you weaken the flesh nature in you so that sin literally starves to death in your life?**

3. <u>Recognize the consequences of giving in to temptation.</u> A hit country music song has a line in it that says "When I think about cheating, I just think about you leaving".
How can thinking about possible consequences help you resist temptation?

4. <u>Accept accountability.</u> If you are really going to grow spiritually, you need to find an accountability partner or group.
How does having a person who will tell you the truth and encourage you help you to grow?

Prayer Connection:

This is the time to encourage, support, and pray for each other in our journeys to learn to hear from God.

Share prayer needs with the group, especially those that are related to hearing from God. Your group facilitator will close your time in prayer.

Prayer Needs:

11

Remember your "Get Ready" daily Bible readings and questions at the beginning of Session 12.

Now What?

Go a little deeper with God in your spiritual journey by completing one of these assignments this week.

Challenge:

Fast for strength. Consider doing some type of fast to begin starving a sin that has driven you crazy. It can be a fast from movies, entertainment, music, food, cokes or whatever. The key is to pray about the issue you are confronting every time you are hungry or would normally be doing the thing you are fasting from. Keep a journal of what you learn and the progress you make.

Bible Reference Notes

Use these notes to deepen your understanding as you study the Bible on your own:

James 1:12

perseveres under trial. This verse is connected to the preceding verses on trials, not to the verses that follow about temptation, given the use of "perseverance" in verses 3, 4, and 12. Perseverance is the desired response to tests, while resistance is the desired response to temptation.
stood the test. The Greek word *dokimos* describes the successful testing of precious metals and coins. It speaks of the process of testing and subsequent approval. Some versions of the Bible translate dokimos as "once he has been approved."
the crown of life. This refers to a wreath placed on the head of a victorious athlete or military leader (2 Tim. 4:8; 1 Pet. 5:4; Rev. 2:10). According to scholars, James is speaking of the believer's future heavenly reward, eternal life. Some commentators, however, insist that since the crown is given as an accomplishment for perseverance following conversion (perseverance prior to conversion would be irrelevant), the verse must refer to a higher quality of life now.

James 1:13

God cannot be tempted by evil. Because of God's holiness, He cannot be tempted. He has no moral depravity to which temptation would appeal.

James 1:14

dragged away and enticed. Greek verbs taken from fishing, perhaps better rendered "drawn out," describing a fish drawn out of its retreat by the sight and/or scent of bait. Sportsmen often bait hunting traps and fishing hooks. The trap or hook must be hidden and the bait most prominent. Temptation thrives upon our natural desire for the bait, all the while concealing the deadly steel trap and sharp metal hook.

James 1:15

desire has conceived. James switches metaphors to that of conception and birth and offers a genealogy of sin. First generation is desire or lust, like a woman who becomes pregnant. This portrays yielding to temptation.
gives birth to sin. As a baby is the result of pregnancy, sin is the result of yielding to temptation.
sin, when it is full-grown, gives birth to death. Sin develops until it is full-grown and well-established and ready to produce offspring (the third generation). Sin produces a baby named "spiritual death." The generations of desire, sin, and death are seen in the temptations of Eve (Gen. 3:6–22) and David (2 Sam. 11:2–17).

Session

12

OVER THE TOP: OVERCOMING DOUBT

Get Ready

Read one of these short Bible passages each day and spend a few minutes wrapping your brain around it. Be sure to jot down any insights you discover.

MONDAY

Read Matthew 11:2-3

Why did John start to question Jesus' identity? What role can trials play in doubting?

TUESDAY

Read Matthew 11:4-5

How did Jesus reassure John? What renews your faith and courage the most in times of doubt?

WEDNESDAY

Read Matthew 11:6

How does it affect your faith to question God about His reasons for allowing some less-that-desirable circumstances in your life?

THURSDAY

Read Exodus 4:10-17

In this passage, Moses doubts that he can do what God is asking. When was the last time you sensed God prompting you to do something you didn't feel qualified to do?

FRIDAY

Read Judges 6:11-18

Gideon wants a sign from God so that he will know that it was actually God who was speaking to him. Would a sign from God increase your faith? Why or why not?

SATURDAY

Read Mark 9:19-25

Think of a time when you felt like this father who says, "I believe" and then turns around and says, "Help my unbelief"?

SUNDAY

Read James 1:5-8

James says in this passage, "the doubter is like the surging sea, driven and tossed by the wind." How can you avoid being an indecisive or passive man or woman?

LifePoint

Doubt is a normal part of the Christian experience. There is always the possibility that we will balk at believing without reservation or act with hesitation. But through faith you can loosen doubt's hold.

SMALL-GROUP TIME: Divide into smaller groups of 4-8, preferably in a circle. You will have a small-group leader for "Say What?"

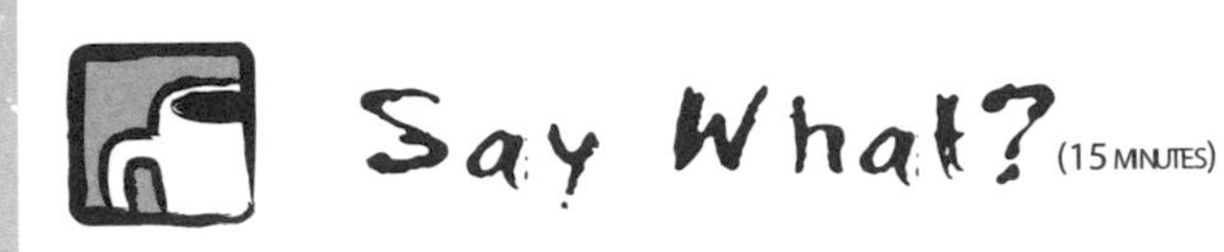

Random Question of the Week:

What is your favorite ice cream flavor?

Group Experience: I Doubt It

You will find examples of advertisements in magazines and newspapers.

After the activity, answer the following questions:

1. What makes you doubt things that you read or see in the media?

2. How can doubting be a positive, or productive, part of the learning process?

3. Describe a time when you doubted something but later discovered it to be true. What was it like when you realized your mistake?

12

LARGE-GROUP TIME: Turn to face the front for this teaching time. Follow along and take notes in your *Student Books.*

So What? (30 MINUTES)

Overcoming Doubt

1. Doubt is a ____________ and _______________ part of our spiritual growth.

2. What is it about God that probably contributes to our struggle with doubt?

Learning from the Bible ...

Matthew 11:2-6

Learning from the Bible

[2] When John heard in prison what the • Messiah was doing, he sent [a message] by his disciples [3] and asked Him, "Are You the One who is to come, or should we expect someone else?"

[4] Jesus replied to them, "Go and report to John what you hear and see: [5] the blind see, the lame walk, those with skin diseases are healed, the deaf hear, the dead are raised, and the poor are told the good news. [6] And if anyone is not offended because of Me, he is blessed."

LARGE-GROUP TIME: Your leader will share some key points with you. Follow along and take notes in your *Student Books.*

Three Spiritual Arenas Where Faith and Doubt Battle

3. Faith and doubt do battle in our lives when we doubt God's _______________, _________________, and_________________.

4. What reasons did John the Baptist have for experiencing moments of doubt?

5. List two biblical figures and their doubts as revealed in the Bible.

6. How did Jesus respond to John's doubts about Him? Why is this important to you?

A Timing Issue

7. What are two ways that the issue of timing can cause us to doubt?

Dealing With Doubt

8. What are five ways to combat doubt in your life?

SMALL-GROUP TIME: **Small-group leaders will direct your discussions. Everyone will gain more if you are open and honest in responding to questions.**

Do What? (15 MINUTES)

1. What type of doubt do you deal with the most?
   - ☐ God's existence
   - ☐ God's unconditional love
   - ☐ God's plans
   - ☐ God's power
   - ☐ God's faithfulness
   - ☐ God's wisdom
   - ☐ God's justice
   - ☐ Other: ______________________

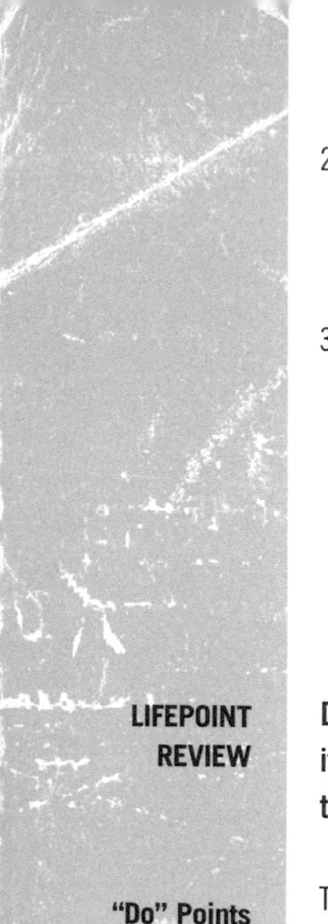

2. What strategy for overcoming this doubt do you think would be most effective?

3. What are the negative consequences that might result from failing to deal with this doubt?

LIFEPOINT REVIEW

Doubt is a normal part of the Christian experience. There is always the possibility that we will balk at believing without reservation or act with hesitation. But through faith you can loosen doubt's hold.

"Do" Points

These "Do" Points will help you grab hold of this week's LifePoint. Be open and honest as you answer the questions within your small group.

1. Identify the kind of doubt. It is important to know what you're specifically dealing with.
   What questions can you ask yourself to help you to discover the type of doubt you have?

2. Confess your doubts to God and ask Him for help. You can't do it on your own.
   Why do you think you need to confess your doubt to God and ask for His help?

3. Turn to God's Word when you're confronted with doubt. The most powerful weapon against a lie is the truth.
   How can Scripture help you defeat doubt?

Prayer Connection:

This is the time to encourage, support and pray for each other in our journeys to learn to hear from God.

Share prayer needs with the group, especially those that are related to hearing from God. Your group facilitator will close your time in prayer.

Prayer Needs:

Remember your "Get Ready" daily Bible readings and questions at the beginning of Session 13 (the last session in this study).

Now What?

Go a little deeper with God in your spiritual journey by completing one of these assignments this week.

Challenge:

Claim promises found in the Bible. List any doubts that you are currently battling. Find verses that apply to these doubts and list them beside each one. Put the verses on cards and read them several times a day until you have committed them to memory.

Bible Reference Notes

Use these notes to deepen your understanding as you study the Bible on your own:

Matthew 11:2

John. John the Baptist, the son of Zechariah and Elizabeth, was the cousin of Jesus. The son of a priest, John forsook the comforts of the priesthood in the city to accept God's call to be a prophet in the wilderness and the forerunner to the Messiah. John pronounced upon Jesus the title "Lamb of God" and released some of his own disciples to follow Him (John 1:29–42). Jesus insisted that John baptize Him despite John's humble protest.
heard in prison. The circumstances surrounding John's imprisonment by Herod are recorded in Matthew 14:3–5.
what Christ was doing. This included reports of Christ's miracles, teaching, and growing mission.
sent his disciples. Those who had been his disciples prior to his imprisonment. We do not know their names, and it is reasonable to think some of the original group may have been frightened away or discouraged by the imprisonment. This sending of disciples suggests that John was permitted to have visitors on occasion.

Matthew 11:3

Are you the one ... or should we expect someone else? John, the prophet, had announced the coming of the Messiah and later pronounced Jesus to be that Messiah. However, John had been in captivity for months, and the works of Jesus had not produced the results that John apparently expected. John had doubts and was seeking reassurance and perhaps wanted Jesus to take further action to usher in the messianic kingdom, including delivering Israel from the oppression of Rome.

Matthew 11:4-5

report to John ... and the good news is preached to the poor. Jesus answered with the evidence of supernatural power, summarizing his own miracles and preaching, voicing it in the Messianic language found in Isaiah 25:5–6; 26:1. It must be noticed that early in his ministry Jesus went into the Nazareth synagogue, stood to read from the scroll Isaiah 61:1–2, and then announced, "Today this Scripture is fulfilled in your hearing" (Luke 4:21). This pronouncement early in His ministry followed by the repeated reference in Matthew 11 resounds as a confirmation of Christ's mission. To put it bluntly, Jesus was saying, "I am doing what I said from the beginning that I came to do." Jesus' purpose was to reassure John that he need not doubt Jesus' identity as Messiah, nor question Jesus' messianic agenda.

Matthew 11:6

Blessed is the man who does not fall away on account of me. The word *skandalizo* in Greek means, "I obstruct another's path." Thus, the verse expresses the position that fortunate is the man who does not find in Jesus an obstacle to belief and subsequently reject Him. Jesus did not want John immobilized by doubt and discouragement.

Session

13

DECISION TIME: SERVING GOD WITH MY LIFE

Get Ready

Read one of these short Bible passages each day and spend a few minutes wrapping your brain around it. Be sure to jot down any insights you discover.

MONDAY

Read Matthew 25:14-15

What gifts, talents, or other resources has God entrusted to you?

TUESDAY

Read Matthew 25:16-18

It wasn't very smart for the servant to dig a hole and bury his master's money. What are you doing to increase the value and influence of the gifts and talents God has given you?

WEDNESDAY

Read Matthew 25:19-23

What steps can you take today to hear these words from God: "Well done"?

THURSDAY

Read Matthew 25:24-25

The servant's fears paralyzed him and prevented him from taking action. What fears prevent you from using your talents to serve God?

FRIDAY

Read Matthew 25:26-30

The story doesn't end well for this servant. He was not faithful with what the master had entrusted to him. How faithful are you in the small things that God has given you to do?

SATURDAY

Read Philippians 2:5-7

According to the passage, Jesus "empties" Himself and made Himself a form of a slave so that God's plan for our salvation could come to fruition. Would you say that your attitude toward others is one of humility and servanthood?

SUNDAY

Read 2 Timothy 1:8-9

Paul tells us in this passage that we have been given a holy calling. How do you need the power of God to help you live a holy life?

LifePoint

God has called us and equipped us to change our world through servanthood and by telling others of God's life changing grace.

SMALL-GROUP TIME: Divide into smaller groups of 4-8, preferably in a circle. You will have a small-group leader for "Say What?"

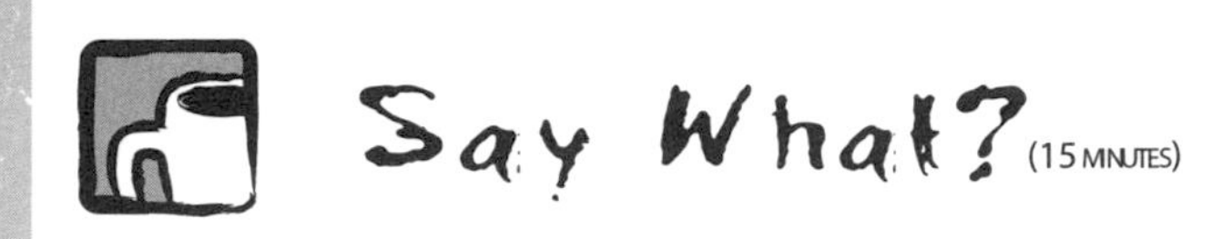

Random Question of the Week:

What is your greatest fear?

1. What are the top three worst jobs you can imagine? Pick from the list or make up your own.
   - ☐ Public relations person for Tom Cruise
   - ☐ Garbage man in New York City
   - ☐ Scriptwriter for "Barney and Friends"
   - ☐ Quality control inspector for canned meat
   - ☐ Proofreader for school textbooks
   - ☐ Massage therapist for injured sumo wrestlers
   - ☐ Other: ______________________________

2. What is your dream job? Why?

3. How do you feel when you have to do something that is really out of character for you?

4. What would be the most humbling experience you could have?

LARGE-GROUP TIME: Turn to face the front for this teaching time. Follow along and take notes in your *Student Books.*

So What? (30 MINUTES)

Serving God With My Life

1. In what specific way did Jesus model the right attitude of a servant? Can you think of others?

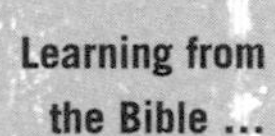

Learning from the Bible ...

Matthew 25:14-30 (NASB)

Learning from the Bible

[14] "For it is just like a man about to go on a journey, who called his own slaves and entrusted his possessions to them. [15] "To one he gave five talents, to another, two, and to another, one, each according to his own ability; and he went on his journey. [16] "Immediately the one who had received the five talents went and traded with them, and gained five more talents. [17] "In the same manner the one who had received the two talents gained two more. [18] "But he who received the one talent went away, and dug a hole in the ground and hid his master's money.

LARGE-GROUP TIME: Your leader will share some key points with you. Follow along and take notes in your *Student Books.*

[19] "Now after a long time the master of those slaves came and settled accounts with them. [20] "The one who had received the five talents came up and brought five more talents, saying, 'Master, you entrusted five talents to me. See, I have gained five more talents.' [21] "His master said to him, 'Well done, good and faithful slave. You were faithful with a few things, I will put you in charge of many things; enter into the joy of your master.'

[22] "Also the one who had received the two talents came up and said, 'Master, you entrusted two talents to me. See, I have gained two more talents.' [23] "His master said to him, 'Well done, good and faithful slave. You were faithful with a few things, I will put you in charge of many things; enter into the joy of your master.'

[24] "And the one also who had received the one talent came up and said, 'Master, I knew you to be a hard man, reaping where you did not sow and gathering where you scattered no seed. [25] 'And I was afraid, and went away and hid your talent in the ground. See, you have what is yours.'

[26] "But his master answered and said to him, 'You wicked, lazy slave, you knew that I reap where I did not sow and gather where I scattered no seed. [27] 'Then you ought to have put my money in the bank, and on my arrival I would have received my money back with interest. [28] 'Therefore take away the talent from him, and give it to the one who has the ten talents.'

[29] "For to everyone who has, more shall be given, and he will have an abundance; but from the one who does not have, even what he does have shall be taken away. [30] "Throw out the worthless slave into the outer darkness; in that place there will be weeping and gnashing of teeth.

Called to Serve

2. What is one of the great wonders of history?

3. Why can't you wait until you've grown up to serve?

The Responsibility of Serving

4. What is the main way that God prepares or equips us to serve Him?

5. Regarding spiritual gifts, what does it mean to put your money to work?

6. In addition to using your spiritual gifts, what other responsibilities do you have?

The Rewards of Faithful Service

7. What are the rewards for faithful service?

    A. An ________________________________ of faithfulness

    B. Additional ________________________________

    C. ________________________________ blessings

13

SMALL-GROUP TIME: Small-group leaders will direct your discussions. Everyone will gain more if you are open and honest in responding to questions.

Do What? (15 MINUTES)

1. Which of the spiritual gifts listed below do you think you may have? Check all that apply.
   - ☐ Prophecy – The ability to speak the truth.
   - ☐ Evangelism – The ability to share the gospel with lost people.
   - ☐ Pastor/Shepherd – The ability to instruct, encourage, and lead a church or small group of believers.
   - ☐ Teaching – The ability to study and communicate biblical truths effectively.
   - ☐ Administration/Leading – The ability to organize projects and lead people.
   - ☐ Exhortation/Encouragement – The ability to comfort, motivate, and counsel wisely.
   - ☐ Faith – The ability to discern God's will and pursue it with extraordinary confidence.
   - ☐ Giving – The ability to contribute material resources to the Lord's work and to people in need with generosity, frequency, and cheerfulness.
   - ☐ Helps/Serving – The ability to assist and support others in practical, behind-the-scenes ways that cause public ministries to run smoothly and effectively.
   - ☐ Showing Mercy – The ability to sense people's needs and hurts and respond to them with comfort and hope.
   - ☐ Hospitality – The ability to open your home and heart to others.

2. What should your response be when you see that some people might have more or different gifts than you?

3. Which reward for faithful service most appeals to you? Why?
   - ☐ Pleasing God
   - ☐ The offer of more opportunities to be used by God
   - ☐ The promise of eternal rewards

LIFEPOINT REVIEW

God has called us and equipped us to change our world through servanthood and by telling others of God's life changing grace.

"Do" Points

These "Do" Points will help you grab hold of this week's LifePoint. Be open and honest as you answer the questions within your small group.

1. Identify your S.H.A.P.E. for ministry. Answer the questions below to help you discover how God has prepared you for ministry.
   · Spiritual Gifts: What are my spiritual gifts?
   · Heart: What kinds of things make me tick?
   · Abilities: What special abilities, skills, and interests do I have?
   · Personality: Am I more of a starter or a responder?
   · Experiences: What are my educational, spiritual, and ministry experiences?
   When will you be able to get by yourself and spend time with God regarding your gifts?

2. Match your S.H.A.P.E. with ministry opportunities. Once you know your gifts, you need to use them.
   What opportunities do you know about in your church or community where you can serve?

3. Commit to developing your gifts in ministry. It is important that you not neglect your spiritual gift.
   How can you develop your gifts?

Prayer Connection:

This is the time to encourage, support, and pray for each other in our journeys to learn to hear from God.

Share prayer needs with the group, especially those that are related to hearing from God. Your group facilitator will close your time in prayer.

Prayer Needs:

Go a little deeper with God in your spiritual journey by completing one of these assignments this week.

Option #1:

Complete a spiritual gifts inventory (ask your youth leaders or pastor for one) and research ways you can use your gifts for service. Ask a friend to make you accountable for getting involved in service this week.

Option #2:

Look up spiritual gifts in your concordance and read about the different gifts and ways they have been used.

Bible Reference Notes

Use these notes to deepen your understanding as you study the Bible on your own:

Matthew 25:14

entrusted his property to them. Some servants in Jesus' day enjoyed considerable responsibility and authority, almost like employees who share in the profits. In this case, property is not real estate but currency.

Matthew 25:15

talents. Estimates var [illegible] ability or gift is derived from [illegible] ***each according to hi*** [illegible] the servants' capabilities [illegible]

Matthew 25:16

put his money to wor [illegible] s venture and worked with [illegible]

Matthew 25:19

the master of those s [illegible] st will return and review our [illegible]

Matthew 25:24

hard man, harvesting [illegible] Should he try t [illegible] ll of the money, h [illegible] ot as important. F [illegible] rdless, he was acc [illegible]

Matthew 25:26

you knew t [illegible] ve the servant's [illegible] he money saf [illegible]

Matthew 25:27

money on [illegible] legal interest w [illegible] 48 percent re [illegible]

Matthew 25:30

throw tha [illegible] to use what [illegible] would set it up a [illegible] The man was [illegible] vard. To me, tha [illegible]

Ackno[illegible]

We since [illegible] outh *Edition.* S [illegible] g this study. We [illegible] iel, Scott Lee [illegible]

GROUP DIRECTORY

PASS THIS DIRECTORY AROUND AND HAVE YOUR GROUP MEMBERS FILL IN THEIR NAMES AND PHONE NUMBERS.

NAME	PHONE